CATHOLIC JEWS AND
THE STATE OF ISRAEL

Studies in Judaism and Christianity

*Exploration of Issues in the
Contemporary Dialogue Between
Christians and Jews*

Editor in Chief for
Stimulus Books
Helga Croner

Editors
Lawrence Boadt, C.S.P.
Helga Croner
David Dalin
Leon Klenicki
John Koenig
Kevin A. Lynch, C.S.P.
Richard C. Sparks, C.S.P.

 A STIMULUS BOOK

CATHOLICS, JEWS AND THE STATE OF ISRAEL

by
Anthony J. Kenny

A STIMULUS BOOK
PAULIST PRESS ◆ NEW YORK ◆ MAHWAH

Library of Congress Cataloging-in-Publication Data

Kenny, Anthony J., 1942–
    Catholics, Jews and the State of Israel / by Anthony J. Kenny.
        p.   cm.—(Stimulus book) (Studies in Judaism and
    Christianity)
    Includes index.
    ISBN 0-8091-3406-3 (pbk.)
        1. Judaism—Relations—Catholic Church.   2. Catholic Church—Relations—
    Judaism.   3. Catholic Church and Zionism.   4. Catholic Church—Foreign
    relations—Israel.   5. Israel—Foreign relations—Catholic Church.
    I. Title.   II. Series.
    BM535.K42   1993
    261.2'6—dc20   93-17833
                                                                              CIP

Published by Paulist Press
997 Macarthur Boulevard
Mahwah, New Jersey 07430

Printed and bound in the United States of America

Contents

Acknowledgments

I owe thanks to many people who have helped me during the time I researched and wrote this work: to Carol, my wife, and Matthew, my son, for their generosity in my long and frequent absences, and for their encouragement, patience and love. To Rabbi Dr. John Levi for his enthusiasm for the subject, his kind and generous friendship, and his wise and learned direction. His supervision of the doctoral thesis from which this text emerged created history: it was, as far as is known, the first time that a Jew had supervised the work of a Catholic candidate for a pontifical doctorate in theology. I wish to thank the Catholic Bishops of Victoria who helped finance my research, and my employer, the Australian Catholic University–Christ Campus for granting me leave in 1988 during which time I was able to consolidate my research in Jerusalem, Rome and London, and the Sisters of Our Lady of Sion, for their lives of witness toward God's abiding covenant-love for his people, the Jews, and for their help and encouragement. I am particularly indebted to those sisters who direct the *Service International de Documentation Judeo-Chrétienne* (SIDIC CENTRE) in Rome, the Centres for Christian-Jewish Relations in London (U.K.) and "Shalom," Kew (Australia). Particular thanks are due to Sister Shirley Sedawie, N.D.S. for reading the manuscript of my work and for her encouragement and immense help. I am grateful to the administration and scholarly community of the *Ecumenical Institute for Advanced Theological Studies,* Tantur, Israel, for their hospitality and help, and for the use of their resources. I also wish to acknowledge the assistance of Sister Rose Thering, O.P. of Seton Hall University, New Jersey, Dr. Eugene Fisher, Executive Secretary of the Secretariat for Catholic-Jewish Relations, Washington, D.C., and Dr. Meir Mendes, former Israeli Minister at the Vatican and Professor at Bar Ilan University, Tel Aviv, Israel. Thanks are also due to Dr. Marie Lawson, The Rev. Professor Robert Anderson, and Mr. Michael Cohen for their help in editing the manuscript.

To
Carol Kristine,

dearest companion
in the journey of life and faith,
thankfully and joyfully marking
our twenty-five years
of marriage

I. Introduction

Over the past thirty years the relationship between the Catholic Church and Jews has radically changed from one of missionary outreach, with the intent to convert Jews, to that of a desire for fraternal fellowship and dialogue of mutual esteem and respect. However, during the past fifteen years a problem focused on the recognition of the State of Israel by the Catholic Church has become a source of very great tension between the two groups. It is a problem which severely threatens the health and even the life of the dialogue.

THE COMMONLY PERCEIVED VIEW
OF THE PROBLEM IN THE DIALOGUE

At a superficial level the problem in the dialogue appears to be of a theological nature. The official Catholic documents relating to the dialogue quite clearly recognize the centrality of the land to Jewish self-understanding and the right of the Jews to a homeland in Israel, but they clearly divorce the State of Israel from this recognition. In the Commission for Religious Relations with the Jews' document *Notes on the correct way to present the Jews and Judaism in preaching and catechesis in the Roman Catholic Church* (June 24, 1985) the authors distinguish between people, land, and the State of Israel. They affirm the Jewish people's attachment to the land and the existence of the State of Israel under international law, but they caution against religious interpretations of the State of Israel.[1]

For Jews, the statement concerning Israel in this document touched an exposed nerve and set off an immediate and volatile reaction which brought forth the strongest possible condemnations from worldwide Jewry, indicating that Jews are beginning to question the good will of the Catholic Church. From this reaction it is clear that most Jews would see

1

the statement about Israel in *Notes on the correct way to present the Jews and Judaism in preaching and catechesis in the Roman Catholic Church* as being anti-Israel and anti-Zionist, and as a product of that form of Christian antisemitism which is rooted in a pseudo-theology which holds that Jews have been rejected and dispossessed of their homeland by God as a punishment for their rejection of the Messiah.

The Holy See has not responded to this Jewish reaction to its Commission's statement nor has it ever explicitly given reasons for the statement. Neither has it ever explained what appears to be either its refusal or its reluctance to establish full de jure diplomatic relations with Israel. Furthermore, whenever Pope John Paul II has been addressed on the issue of Israel by Jews he has always chosen not to respond on the subject. The Holy See's lack of explanation and the Pope's silences are taken by Jews as further evidence of the Catholic Church's disregard for what is the most vital contemporary Jewish concern: the continuing safety and security of the State of Israel. These factors serve to confirm Jewish opinion that there must be a theological basis for perceived Catholic attitudes toward the State of Israel.

Recognition of Israel has been identified as a Catholic problem by a number of Catholic writers who have been deeply involved in the Catholic-Jewish dialogue long before the Commission's statement appeared.

The late *Sister Charlotte Klein, N.D.S.*[2] writes criticizing the silence of the Catholic Church on the issue of the significance of the State of Israel for Jews. She argues that there are theological reasons for this silence and that they arise from the Christian teaching about God's rejection of the Jews seen in the events surrounding the destruction of the Temple in 70 CE.

Klein counsels that in any theological consideration of Israel it would be obligatory to consider Jewish self-interpretation which includes the two essential ingredients, election and the promise of the land, both of which are related to the covenant. It is, she contends, precisely these elements that are so difficult for a Christian theology which tenaciously clings to the doctrine of universal salvation through Christ.

The late *Reverend Cornelius Rijk*[3] reports that the return of the Jews to the land and the creation of the State of Israel, while strengthening the identity of many Jews, comes as a shock to many Christians. Consequently there exists much confusion and much misunderstanding about the link between people, land and religion. Rijk suggests that a too abstract Christian theology of those elements of Judaism has been the cause among Christians of the lack of deeper understanding of their relationship and of their role in the perspective of salvation history.

The Reverend Charles Angell, S.A.,[4] acknowledging the continuing difficulty which the State of Israel poses for the dialogue, indicates two problematic areas which hold back Christian recognition of Israel. First, the many and diverse understandings of Israel that exist among Jews, and, second, the problem of the changing borders of Israel in 1967 and 1973. He believes that the issue would be solved by speaking of the rights of peoples to self-determination rather than their rights to geographical areas.

Others have written since the publication of the Commission's document to explain its statement about Israel and to suggest ways of resolving the problem which the statement has produced in the dialogue.

The Reverend Thomas Stransky, C.S.P.[5] urges the Holy See, which, he observes, acknowledges the validity and necessity of the Jewish State, to exchange formal diplomatic relations with Israel as a clear signal in the international arena that it in no way supports those Arab states which reject even the right of Israel to exist and which insist that by political and military means Israel should be forced to disappear from the Middle East.

Dr. Eugene Fisher[6] explains the Holy See's relationship to Israel as an "evolving attitude." Basically, he argues, there are three areas to be taken into account in this process: first, socio-political implications faced by the Holy See which include her relationships with Israel's neighbors; second, major historical factors involved in Christianity's traditional stake in the Holy Land; third, the extent to which the Church's perception may have been influenced by its past and present theological attitudes toward Jews and Judaism.

Fisher explains that the Holy See's evolving understanding and policy is to be seen in her documentation since 1948, culminating in the Apostolic Letter *Redemptionis Anno* in 1984. Fisher contends that the existence of Israel is unequivocally recognized de jure and de facto on the basis of common principles of international law[7] and notes also the presence of a caveat about fundamentalist religious interpretations.

Fisher argues that Catholics must listen sympathetically and affirmatively to the crucial internal discussions currently taking place within the Jewish community because that will assist Catholics to understand the religious significance of Israel for Jews.

The Reverend Bruce Williams, O.P.[8] explains the "*instinctive*"

Catholic antipathy to Zionism as arising from the political claims of the movement which appear to be incompatible with the Church's own traditional, transhistorical redemptive script for Jews which is that the redemption of Israel must await its conversion at the end of human history after centuries of forced exile in punishment for its rejection of Christ. This attitude is well documented, Williams claims, and one which persists in spite of the work of Vatican II when it was tacitly abandoned. Williams sees it still lurking behind the Holy See's reticence and the *Notes'* ambivalence to the State of Israel.

Williams suggests that the Holy See could immediately dispel an abiding suspicion which clouds the dialogue with Jews by a clarifying reassurance that its political stance toward the State of Israel rests on prudential considerations and not any longer on the old theology of rejection of the Jews. It could go even further than this, Williams asserts, by acknowledging the rebirth of the State of Israel as a sign of the times which carries positive theological meaning for Jews and Christians.

Klein, Rijk, Fisher and Williams confirm the Jewish perspective of the problem of Israel in the dialogue. They assert that Catholic theology, for one reason or another, has great difficulty in accommodating religious recognition of Israel and the events which have surrounded its rebirth.

However, the problem of Israel in the dialogue has never been systematically investigated.[9] It has for a long time been an area of speculation. Its cause or causes are the subject of both Jewish allegations and Christian scholarly assertions. Moreover, the current state of impasse on this issue in the dialogue calls for a thorough and systematic investigation of the problem from both the Jewish and the Catholic perspectives.

THE PROBLEM UNDER CLOSE FOCUS

A systematic investigation of the evidence from both sides of the dialogue would show that the statement relating to Israel in *Notes on the correct way to present the Jews and Judaism in preaching and catechesis in the Roman Catholic Church* (VI, 25) is not the product of a theological problem. It would also reveal that there is no theological reason why the Catholic Church should not give theological recognition to Israel and the events surrounding its rebirth. Such an investigation would also reveal that the problem is of an entirely different nature. It would show that on the Catholic side there exists a flaw in the official dialogical method. It would also reveal that on the Jewish side, on the one hand, there exists a profound hermeneutical problem associated with Israel and, on the other hand, a deep-seated existential insecurity which is inextricably connected with the well-being of the State of Israel. The study would reveal that it is the fusion of the Jewish existential problem and the Catholic methodological flaw that has created the complex problem in the dialogue.

The following systematic investigation of the evidence available from both sides of the dialogue will attempt to refocus the problem.

TERMS WHICH WILL OCCUR FREQUENTLY THROUGHOUT THIS TEXT

In the investigation which follows a number of terms will appear which require prior definition, and they are as follows.

Israel

Use of this term throughout this study refers to that national entity which exists in the territory known as "Israel," and which is incorporated in the territory formerly known as "Palestine." It is that political and national entity which sees itself as the continuation of the Jewish nation, the "Second Jewish Commonwealth," which was finally crushed by the Roman Empire in 135 CE. It is that entity which, in spite of frequent territorial and border changes, came into being by an Act of the United Nations on November 29, 1947, and which was declared on May 15, 1948, at the termination of the British Mandate on May 14, 1948, and which is recognized under international law as a self-determining, democratic political body and nation.

Where the expressions "Israel" and "State of Israel" occur throughout this study, they incorporate the following three elements.

Am Yisrael (People of Israel), that is to say, the Jewish people who trace their roots back to the biblical Hebrew people, either ethnically or theologically, or both.

Eretz Yisrael (Land of Israel), expressed in either theological or secular terms, linking it to the ancient homeland of the biblical Hebrew people and thus, theologically, to the covenant of Genesis 15:1–21. It is the land in which Jews have always maintained a presence, often as a small minority surviving under foreign subjugation.

Medinat Yisrael (State of Israel), which refers to the political form of Jewish civilization in the land at a given period: the First Commonwealth under Joshua, the Judges and the Kings (1250–586 BCE) and the Second Commonwealth under Ezra, the Maccabees, and the Herodians (538 BCE–70 CE); the Third Commonwealth, under the democratically elected leadership of the people, currently known as the "State of Israel" (1948 CE–).

In this study the expressions *State of Israel, Israel, the return of the people to the land* and *the rebirth of the nation-state* are interchangeable.

Jew, Jewish, Judaism

These terms refer to those people who have been born of Hebrew ethnicity or who have, by a religious act, been admitted to the same status as those who have been born of such parents. The designations are inclusive of religious and non-religious, observant and non-observant, believing and non-believing. They include the whole spectrum of Jewish religious expression, in its broadest definition, fundamentalist and non-fundamentalist. They include the particular religious dimensions: Ultra-Orthodoxy, Orthodoxy, Conservatism, Reconstructionism and Reform.

Jews are to be equated with *Am Yisrael* (People of Israel) whether or not they reside in the State of Israel. Jews who live in the State of Israel will be called *Israelis*.

The Catholic-Jewish Dialogue

As a result of the Second Vatican Council the Catholic Church embarked upon a renewed dialogue with Judaism.[10] One commentator on this dialogue remarks:

> Only twenty years ago, with only fifteen long Latin sentences the impossible became possible and the possible became act. 2,221 council fathers by their approval committed the Roman Catholic Church to an irrevocable act, a heshbon ha-nefesh—a reconsideration of soul. The act began to shift with integrity 1,900 years of relationships between Catholics and Jews.[11]

The about-face of Vatican II turned the Catholic Church's relationship with the Jewish people from one of mission and proselytizing toward a fraternal dialogue. This new direction is expressed by the Holy See in the following way:

> Such relations as there have been between Jews and Christians have scarcely ever risen above the level of monologue. From now on, real dialogue must be established.[12]

The contemporary Catholic-Jewish dialogue exists on two related planes.

First there is the "dialogue of love" which is marked by the ordinary day-to-day relationships and fellowship that exists between Christians and Jews. The *Guidelines* (1974) speaks of this when recommending that

> on the practical level in particular, Christians should strive to acquire a better knowledge of the basic components of the religious traditions of Judaism; they must strive to learn by what essential traits Jews define themselves in the light of their own religious experience.[13]

This "dialogue of love" is seen to be operative at person to person, family to family, parish to synagogue levels. It is also apparent in such organizations as the *Council of Christians and Jews,* of which Catholics are members in company with other Christians, and other bodies of mutual fellowship and intellectual exchange.

The other plane on which the dialogue is operative is more official in nature and is marked by the relationship of the Holy See with the leaders of the worldwide Jewish community, especially through the work of the *Commission for Religious Relations with Jews* which was established in 1974 by Pope John Paul II. Prior to this a desk for Jewish-Christian relations was set up in the Secretariat for the Promotion of Christian Unity in 1966 with the Rev. Dr. C.C. Rijk responsible. The theological dialogue is to be seen when national Bishops' Conferences establish committees of official dialogue between Catholics and Jews in local areas. The official theological dialogue manifests itself from time to time in the production of documentation—*Guidelines* (1974) for example—the purpose of which has been to implement the Vatican II Declaration *Nostra Aetate* in the day-to-day life of the Church.

Zionism

Zionism is not only that political movement which developed in the nineteenth century but is essentially *"that profound longing for the full-*

ness of Jewishness which can only be attained by the return of the Jewish people to the land of the promise."[14]

The return to Zion is that eventuality for which the Rabbis began to prepare immediately after the destruction of Jerusalem by the Romans in 135 CE, and for which every pious Jew in every generation down to our own has prayed ever since that event. From that time the Rabbis of the first and second centuries CE built a new expression of religious being for their people which would allow them to maintain their lives oriented to the Torah and to survive until the new exile had come to an end, the Temple had been rebuilt, and once again they would settle their homeland, Holy Zion, the land of the promise. The Talmud, comprising Mishnah and Gemarah, is the product of the Rabbis' work. There we find that the ordinary Jewish people have become the center of the cultus: the Jewish household, the common meal, the relationships between peoples. Thus the holiness of Israel would survive in the face of calamity and exile until it could be re-established in Zion, in the land of the promise.[15] A study of the Jewish liturgical life which developed during these times reveals that the land (and its synonyms, "Holy Zion," "Jerusalem," "The Return") is in the foremost consciousness of Jewish religious life. From the smallest liturgical act, the grace before meals, to the greatest liturgical feast, "*Jerusalem*" is constantly on the lips of Jewish people.

The longing for the end of exile and the return to Zion has been productive of a complex Zionist mythology which has become the basis of modern Zionist ideology, whether secular or religious. Basically, this implies the theological and/or historic right to the land and to a state, the end of exile from the Jewish homeland ("Palestine" in Roman time; "Terra Sancta" during the Byzantine Era until the British Mandate in 1917 when "Palestine" was again revived), and the ingathering or "redemption" (if theologically expressed) of the Jewish people.

Zionism, expressed in sheer secular terms, implies the reunification of the three elements, *people, land, state*. In religious terms the implications are the same, but the reunification is expressed in the language of messianism.

The Magisterium

The expression "Magisterium" refers to the authoritative office and ministry of teaching in the Catholic Church which the Lord Jesus Christ gave to the apostles and to their successors, the popes and the bishops.

This is a ministry which is aimed at the correct proclamation of the Gospel, the building up within the Body of Christ, the Church, of love and service, of the proper administration of the sacraments and other matters spiritual and moral.

It is not a ministry/authority to teach abstract doctrines for their own sake, but rather a ministry/authority which is the means or guarantee under the guidance of the Holy Spirit of transmitting and addressing the saving word of Jesus Christ to every generation. Under the Holy Spirit, this ministry/authority maintains historical continuity with Jesus Christ.

The ministry of the Magisterium operates at two levels. The Ordinary Magisterium is the ministry/authority exercised by the Pope and Bishops through their ordinary teaching office which is commonly encountered in homilies, pastoral letters, encyclicals and the like. The Extraordinary Magisterium, as implied by the name, is teaching arising from the ordinary day-to-day sphere. It is exercised by the Pope when he solemnly defines a matter of faith or morals and speaks "ex cathedra," that is, from Peter's chair. The bishops gathered at an ecumenical or general Council of the Church in union with the Pope can also solemnly define a matter of Faith or Morals. Teachings so defined are called Dogmas of the Faith.

The Magisterium is a ministry recognized by all Catholics. It is exercised on behalf of the Lord Jesus Christ under the guidance of the Holy Spirit.

The Holy See

The Holy See is the Catholic Diocese of Rome which is of Apostolic foundation and which, therefore, is designated "Holy." Its Bishop, the Pope, is recognized by Catholics as the successor of the Apostle Peter. The function of the Holy See through its Bishop and his administration is primarily a religious service to the Roman Church and to the Universal Church.

By the Lateran Treaty and Concordat (1929) the Italian Government recognizes the independent sovereignty, under the Pope and his administration, of that section of the Diocese of Rome known as "the Vatican," and its official designation is *Stato della Citta del Vaticano.* The functional distinctions between the Holy See and the Vatican State are blurred by common reference to the Holy See as "the Vatican."

II. The Problem for Jews: Defining Jews in Christian Perspectives

The initial step in our investigation will be to assess from a Jewish perspective, by a study of literature from Jewish sources, the perceived nature of the problem associated with Israel in the Catholic-Jewish Dialogue.

THE ORIGINS OF THE PROBLEM

For the Jewish community the problem associated with the State of Israel and the Catholic Church began to develop its larger dimension after the publication of the *Guidelines* (*1974*) with its total silence on the State of Israel and the significance of this for contemporary Jewry.[1] Typical of the disappointment among Jews over this omission is the statement of the Chief Rabbi of Paris, *Meyer Jais:*

> *(Jews)* . . . are unanimous in interpreting the complete silence of the Council's Declaration and of the Roman document on the historical and religious bonds between the Jewish people and the Holy Land as proof of the total absence of any significant change in the Church's new outlook on Judaism.[2]

This documentary silence, in conjunction with the silence of the Catholic Church at the time of the Six Day War in 1967 and the Yom Kippur War in 1973, inflicted a deep wound in the corporate Jewish psyche which would painfully grow[3] until the publication of the *Notes on the Correct Way To Present the Jews and Judaism in Preaching and Catechesis in the Roman Catholic Church* in 1985, which brought things to a head. In that document is found the statement that

Christians are invited to understand this religious attachment which finds its roots in biblical tradition, without, however, making their own any particular religious interpretation of this relationship (cf. Declaration of U.S. Conference of Catholic Bishops, November 20, 1975).

The existence of the State of Israel and its political options should be envisaged not in a perspective which is in itself religious, but in their reference to the common principles of international law.[4]

This statement has been productive of much dissatisfaction in the worldwide Jewish community. In Australia, *Rabbi Raymond Apple* of the Great Synagogue in Sydney published an *Open Letter to the Pope* in which he said:

> The second problem [in Notes] has accompanied all the recent documents and expressions of new emphasis. The earlier documents (Nostra Aetate and Guidelines [1974]) ignored the existence of the State of Israel; the latest notes (i.e. Notes) acknowledge Jewish attachment to the holy land but stress that Israel must not be understood in religious but political terms.

> Conversation with Judaism, to be open and honest, *cannot* refuse to recognize what it is that Judaism and Jews see in Israel. The fact that it is a political State is only one aspect of Israel as understood by Jews and in Judaism. Every page of the Jewish prayer book breathes the spirit of Zionism, every age in Jewish history has cherished the hope for the restoration of the people of Israel to the land of Israel; Jewish messianism has always expected regained Jewish independence in Israel as indispensable in the final fulfilment of Biblical prophecy. To remove the religious dimension from the Jewish attachment to Israel is to distort Judaism and, I am afraid, to commit a new act of inaccuracy which bodes ill for future conversations between the Church and the Jewish people.[5]

After *Notes'* publication a number of international Jewish assemblies and individual Jewish leaders made vociferous criticisms. Among these criticisms were serious allegations about the sincerity, motives and intentions of the Catholic Church. Some shed doubt on the future of the dialogue.

JEWISH RESPONSES AND REACTIONS TO THE
TREATMENT OF THE STATE OF ISRAEL IN NOTES

The following body of opinion from Jewish leaders, focusing mainly on this statement in *Notes,* suggests various reasons for the putative non-recognition of the State of Israel by the Catholic Church, and it also highlights various issues which Jews associate with that putative non-recognition.

Official Jewish Assemblies Speak Out

Soon after the publication of *Notes* three important international Jewish assemblies took up the issue of the document's statement about Israel, linking it with the fact that the Holy See has no full de jure diplomatic relations with Israel.

The *International Jewish Committee on Interreligious Consultations* (*IJCIC*)[6] seriously criticized the document for defining Jews by Christian categories. Israel, it complained, is emptied of any possible significance for Christians by the publication. Furthermore it noted that the State's profound religious significance for Jews is mentioned in such recondite fashion as to make it unrecognizable. As a result the Committee concluded that this document, which was meant as a teaching aid, was totally inadequate to provide any understanding on the vital issue of Jewish existence because contemporary Jewish existence is decisively shaped by the existence of the State of Israel.

At the fiftieth anniversary of the *World Jewish Congress*[7] the Chairman of one of its sub-committees (the *Commission on Interreligious Affairs*), *Henry Siegman,* in the key address told the Assembly that the Holy See's reluctance to establish diplomatic relations with Israel is the consequence, at least in part, of certain residual and unacknowledged influences that betray an ancient theological sensitivity which sees in a reborn Jewish sovereignty a challenge to the classical Christian notion that Jewish homelessness and exile are inexorable consequences of its rejection of the Christian Messiah. Siegman acknowledges that any theological basis for not recognizing the State of Israel is denied by the Church, but he argues that all the Church documentation prior to and including *Notes* has made it impossible to accept the Church's denial.

Nevertheless Siegman is happy with the formulation as it stands in *Notes.* He is pleased to have Israel recognized only on the basis of international law because he believes that any doctrinal significance should play no role whatever in the secular international arena of a religiously pluralistic world. He also stresses that only common principles of international law should apply. To argue for the admissibility of theological considerations would be, he claimed, to argue for the Crusades or the Inquisition or a Khomeini-type of holy war. But even so, Siegman continues, this does not absolve the Holy See for withholding, for whatever other political consideration, de jure relations with Israel.

Siegman believes that the Holy See's excuse about withholding relationships with nations which have border disputes is pathetic. He points to the fact of the Holy See's full diplomatic relationships with Germany right up until May 1945, through all that time when its borders were changing frequently. The truth, Siegman claims, is that the Holy See maintains formal relationships with all kinds of nations that have unresolved border disputes with their neighbors, even those which are guilty of the most egregious violations of human rights. Why then, he asks, is the Holy See selective in the case of Israel? Siegman thus implies antisemitism.

The *World Jewish Congress* expressed its attitude in a letter sent to all member communities and organizations. There it claimed that, in spite of all the progress made since *Nostra Aetate* in 1965, no amount of rhapsodizing about accomplishments registered twenty years ago could obscure the sad reality that the Catholic Church remains unwilling to accept the fundamental assertion of Jewish national identity focused in the birth of Israel. The authors stressed that the Church must understand that Jews are ultimately united in the view that normalization of relations with all Jews includes that one-quarter of the Jewish people who live in Israel. Through its letter the Congress launched a global campaign for de jure recognition of Israel by the Holy See:

> It is essential that those Jews who represent the Jewish people and who are in meetings with the Pope or with representatives of the Holy See, raise with increased vigour the subject of diplomatic recognition. This should be the first item on the agenda at any meeting.

These international Jewish bodies are concerned that the Catholic Church does not understand or refuses to understand the profound significance which Jews claim for the State of Israel. This is clearly seen by them as a grave problem in the dialogue.

Some of the authors of these statements specify that Israel has a religious and theological significance, although none of them elaborate on the meaning of this claim. All three organizations register their distress at what they perceive to be either the reluctance or the refusal of the Holy See to establish full de jure political relations with Israel, which they regard as being imperative. However, none of the organizations give clear reasons for the urgency of their demands.

Siegman alone ventures, by guessing it seems, to explore the motives of the Holy See's refusal and he attributes this to a theological problem for which he implies an antisemitic basis.

Addresses by Jewish Leaders to Pope John Paul II

Thereafter, the suggestion of the *World Jewish Congress* to pursue diplomatic recognition with officials of the Holy See was assiduously acted upon by those representatives of Jewish organizations and committees who had access to audiences with Pope John Paul II, as the following examples show.

Howard Friedman,[8] President of the American Jewish Committee, spoke to the Pope about the Jewish conviction that the primary obstacle to peace in the Middle East is the ongoing illusion held by most of Israel's neighbors that somehow by withholding formal recognition of Israel's sovereign legitimacy her continued existence can be undermined. Nothing, Friedman asserted, would contribute more to peace than dispelling that illusion. That is why the world Jewish community holds that full de jure political recognition is so vital. The establishment of diplomatic ties would also, he claimed, be a watershed in Catholic-Jewish relations. It would be considered by Jews a happy development and confirmation of the work of Vatican II. However, above all these things, suggests Friedman, the establishment of diplomatic ties would be an act of profound spiritual and ethical significance in advancing the cause of world peace and would help to create the sense of reality which is indispensable to peace.

Mordecai Waxman,[9] at that time Chairman of *IJCIC*, reminded the Pope that in recent years the Jewish people had been undergoing a profound transformation. First, he claimed, the Holocaust shook them to the roots of their being, and then the creation of Israel restored them religiously and spiritually as a factor of history. For the third time in history, Waxman asserted, the pattern of exile and redemption had been re-enacted with great implications which confirm the biblical belief that the Covenant with the land endures even as the Covenant of the Torah endures.

At the Roman Synagogue the Chief Rabbi *Elio Toaff*[10] spoke to the Pope about the significance of the return of the Jews to the Promised

Land. The return, *"the beginning of the coming of final redemption,"* said the Rabbi, must be recognized as a beneficial and inalienable gain for the world because it contributed to that foretold prelude to the epoch of universal brotherhood to which all people aspire, and also to the biblical promise of redemptive peace. The Rabbi asserted that the recognition of Israel's irreplaceable role in the final plan of redemption that God has promised cannot be denied.

In his address to the Pope the President of the Jewish Community in Rome, *Giacomo Saban,*[11] asked for the abandonment of *"certain reticences regarding the State of Israel."* He reminded the Pope that the land of Israel has a role that is central, emotionally and spiritually, in the heart of every Jew, and he suggested that a change of the Holy See's attitude toward Israel would gratify all Jews worldwide, as it would also make a real contribution to the pacification of the Middle East. Such a change of attitude, Saban claimed, would be a further step in the fraternal dialogue of which *Nostra Aetate* speaks.

These Jewish leaders are not commenting directly on *Notes,* but their speeches reflect that foremost of Jewish concerns, the recognition of the existence of the State of Israel and, in particular, its recognition by the Catholic Church. Their concerns are motivated by deeply felt fears for Israel's security.

Each of the speakers focuses on the reticence of the Holy See to establish full de jure diplomatic ties with Israel. The considerations which they give for this request are varied and include the establishment of world peace and the security of Israel's future (Friedman), religious considerations (Waxman and Toaff), the centrality of Israel to the hearts of all Jews (Saban), and the completion of the work of Vatican II (Friedman, Saban).

Press Comments

The tone of reports in the press is much more terse.

Lord Immanuel Jakobovits,[12] Orthodox Chief Rabbi of Great Britain and Northern Ireland, speaks of the disturbing and painfully casual nature of *Notes'* reference to the State of Israel and the Holocaust. The Church, he noted, continued to deny any formal recognition or religious significance to the State. This is an attitude, asserted Jakobovits, now shared only by Arabs, Communists and some other hostile states.

The Chairman of the Executive Committee of the International Council of Christians and Jews, *Sir Sigmund Sternberg,*[13] argues that the fact that the Holy See still does not recognize the State of Israel is a sign that *"in this central area, Jewish self-understanding is regarded lightly."* Sir Sigmund concluded that there was still much more to be done at the grass roots level, and that *"the effort can be made only by Catholics."*

Rabbi Professor Arthur Hertzberg,[14] a Vice-President of the World Jewish Congress, writes that there is something very wrong with the dialogue between Catholics and Jews. For twenty years, he contends, the Catholic Church has used every tactic to avoid the issue that matters most to world Jewry: the recognition of Israel. He reports that at meetings between the dialogue partners the Holy See makes much of denouncing antisemitism, but the very thing that matters to Jews it ignores. Yet, he continues, this attitude toward Israel is not a new problem. It can be seen as far back in history as the encounter of Theodor Herzl with Pope Pius X in 1904. Successive Popes have expressed sympathy with the humanitarian aspects of Zionism, but they have always looked toward the conversion of the Jews. The Church, he complains, will simply not accept the notion that world Jewry, like the Church itself, has temporal as well as spiritual concerns, for *"they want to treat us as a purely spiritual entity so that they can avoid dealing with the issue that matters most to us, explicit recognition of Israel."* For Jews, even the most secular, Hertzberg explains, the return to Zion is a culminating moment in their history, and they will therefore show serious displeasure at any hint that Israel's existence is questionable on theological grounds. He emphasizes that the dialogue cannot go on forever fueled on promises, no more than the Holy See can be allowed to plead for more time on the issue of Israel while at the same time enhancing the status of the Palestinian Liberation Organization. The relationship with world Jewry requires a new beginning, he insists, with a foundation which includes temporal concerns of Judaism, and this, he adds, means that Israel must be at the top of the agenda.

From Israel *Professor Wilikovsky,*[15] President of the Hebrew Israeli Committee for Interreligious Consultations, complained that *Notes* did not take the significance of Israel properly into account.

The editor of the *Jerusalem Post*[16] regretted that what he saw in *Notes* was a retrograde step in the fundamental theological question. In his view the document made the Jews lose their basic dignity.

From Canada *Andre Elbaz*[17] wrote that even though the Holy See has not yet recognized the State of Israel, the Jewish people have always been obliged to recognize the temporal power of the Church. Consequently, he contends, to adopt an ostrich-like policy would be ill-advised.

The problem of the recognition of Israel by the Catholic Church again emerges clearly into focus from this literature.

In these reports we can detect tones of exasperation, frustration, suspicion, hurt, and an acute sense of insecurity relating to the future of the State of Israel. Emotions run high and so do allegations and assertions. Very clearly the authors regard the situation as they perceive it, politically and theologically, with great seriousness, and they view the initiative for the improvement of this matter to rest solely with the Catholic Church.

Journals and Reviews on the Issue

There has been a sprinkling of articles by Jewish critics of the dialogue published in scholarly journals and reviews since the publication of *Notes*. The following are the views of representative and well-known Jewish figures who are engaged in the dialogue with the Catholic Church.

Rabbi Dr. Arthur Hertzberg,[18] reflecting on *Notes,* writes that he believes that the dialogue has reached its theoretical limit, that no further change is possible. He thinks that Catholics and Jews will continue to be disappointed in their deepest expectations of the dialogue. Hertzberg believes that Catholics respect Judaism only because it is part of the religious history of Christianity. He holds that Christianity at its deepest level continues to grapple with its age-old problem of the Jewish rejection of the "new dispensation." On the other hand Jews, he writes, have concluded that twenty years of dialogue and of pushing Christians toward formal recognition of Israel have ended in total disappointment. Jews have wanted Catholics to think of Judaism on its own terms and not on the terms of Catholic theology. Hertzberg concludes that dimensions of people, history and land, all of the factors which unite believing Jews with disbelieving Jews, mean nothing to Catholics and that they simply escape through the lines of the Catholic documents. Hertzberg thinks that the Holy See's interests in the Middle East are greater than her interests in the dialogue and that they preclude any possibility of extending formal recognition to Israel. The Church, he claims, cloaks its dealings with the Arab world by repeating its condemnations of antisemitism, and, he avers, this will continue to be the case.

Rabbi Dr. Norman Solomon[19] sets out to indicate a range of problems and opinions in his commentary on *Notes*. He sees a fundamental problem in the fact that though the document was in preparation for some years, it was placed into the hands of Jewish consultants only ten days prior to its publication. In effect, he claims, there was no consultation. He then turns to an evaluation of the document, giving fair criticism and fair praise. Solomon asks whether it is *"possible for Christians to meet Jews as normal human beings rather than as peculiar theological problems."* In this way Solomon effectively moves the issue of the recognition past the theological arena and directly to the more open one of international law. He holds that the Holy See is right in directing Christians to understand Israel by the principle of international law. His concern is that theological interpretations given to Israel might prove problematical at the least, and at the worst inimical to Jewish aspirations.

Solomon dismisses the criticisms which Jakobovits, Sternberg, Hertzberg and the International Jewish Committee on Interreligious Consultation make about the dialogue. He pleads: *"Please get on with the job of establishing relations, but do not let it* [Israel] *any longer impede progress of your theological dialogue."*

In the opinion of *Rabbi Emanuel Rackman*,[20] President of Bar Ilan University in Israel, the failure of the Catholic Church to recognize Israel makes Jews doubt that the Catholic documentation is anything more than a profession of love with the usual innocuous consequences that flow from such professions, as distinguished from legally consequential acts that alter the relationships of parties.

Rackman argues that the creation of the State of Israel was a momentary response of conscience to the Holocaust on the part of the USA and USSR, and that the fact that the Holy See did not join them, for whatever reason, indicates that these two secular states have a keener conscience than the very power most responsible for the antisemitism that made the Holocaust possible.

To remain neutral vis-à-vis the Zionist claims and aspirations, Rackman asserts, is to make a mockery of justice and peace which are so often spoken of in the Catholic documentation. Neutrality, he claims, aids and abets and encourages terrorists.

Rackman concludes that recognition of the State of Israel by the Holy See is not only warranted but even mandated. He believes that Jews will have to wait for a long time for the fulfillment of that for which they had hoped from *Nostra Aetate*.

In a highly positive appraisal of the Catholic Church's role in the dialogue and of the documentation and theological progress that has marked it, *Dr Gerhardt Riegner*[21] refutes the view of Rabbi Hertzberg that the dialogue is really at the end of the road. Riegner believes, on the contrary, that it has a long way to go into the future. He nevertheless writes critically about the deficiencies of the dialogue, offering useful data for its future reflection. One of the three areas discussed is Israel. While acknowledging Israel for the first time, *Notes* raises some questions of a very deep nature for Jews. Yet, Riegner claims, the answers can only be given by Christians, and these answers will not be easy. How, for instance, can the document ask Christians to understand the religious nature of the land based on biblical tradition without making it their own interpretation of Scripture and the confirmation of the unbroken validity of the "Old Testament" whose central point was the promise of the land? Riegner comments that the Holy See had good opportunities to present the Jewish view on this matter during the political crises in the Middle East but that it failed to do so because "*our positions in this matter are far apart.*"

In these responses we can recognize many of the comments, criticisms and issues that we have seen previously. Some writers (Hertzberg and Rackman) purvey particularly pessimistic views of the dialogue and the Catholic Church's role in it, while others (Solomon and Riegner) maintain their optimism for the dialogue. Some allegations have been made about the Holy See's motivations and interests. These have political and religious implications and all are of a serious nature. They demand further investigation.

REVIEWING THE JEWISH OPINION

It is clear from these reports that all of the Jewish leaders whose opinions were investigated agree that there is a problem in the official Catholic-Jewish dialogue which is centered on Israel and its recognition by the Catholic Church and which is straining relationships between these two religious traditions to a serious degree.

The problem from the Jewish perspective is composed of two elements, the first of which is the immediate or efficient cause of the various reactions which have been examined above, and the second, an underlying or remote cause, a long-standing irritant for Jews.

The efficient cause of the reactions is the statement concerning the State of Israel in *Notes* which, as we have observed in the reports, is plainly offensive to many Jews. Many Jews, as we have seen, read the statement as a sign that the Catholic Church has a fundamental problem in recognizing Israel. They interpret the problem as being of a theological nature. Furthermore, and more seriously for the dialogue itself, the statement is also interpreted by Jews as a sign that the Catholic Church dismisses Jewish sensibilities on this issue by refusing to acknowledge Israel as a reality indivisibly linked to the well-being of contemporary Jewish existence. Through their many expressions of dissatisfaction, Jewish authorities have indicated that acceptance of Israel as primarily and vitally important for contemporary Jews by the Catholic Church is a *sine qua non* for the future of dialogue and that there is no room whatever for negotiation on this issue.

Jews want the Catholic Church to understand that it is a distortion of reality to give a notional recognition of the centrality of the land for Jewish self-identity which is separated from the State of Israel. Divorcing the idea of a homeland from the State as *Notes* does gives no recognition of the reality of the Jewish people as they exist in the contemporary world. Jews want the Catholic Church to understand that recognition of the contemporary reality of Judaism means seeing Jews as they are in the contemporary world, with Israel at the center of their existence.

The reality which these Jewish leaders want recognized is that Jewish peoplehood and the State of Israel are, from May 15, 1948, existentially one and the same thing. Recognition of contemporary Judaism necessarily means accepting this reality. It is this reality which distinguishes contemporary Jewish existence and which delineates it from Jewish existence prior to the re-establishment of the Jewish State in 1948.

Notes' direction that Christians *"should refrain from making their own any particular religious interpretation"* of the State of Israel and that they should interpret it only *"by reference to the common principles of international law"* appears to many leading Jews as a contradiction of what the Holy See had promoted as a fundamental method of dialogue in *Guidelines (1974),* which stressed that *"Christians should strive to learn by what essential traits Jews define themselves in the light of their own religious experience"*[22] (emphasis added).

For Jews, *Notes'* caveat fosters a false view of Jewish existence. It directs Christians to focus on notions rather than on the reality of contemporary Jewish existence.

The statement in *Notes* provokes Jews to ask serious questions. Why has the State of Israel, as fundamental to contemporary Jewish existence, been made an exception to *Guidelines'* (*1974*) clear instruction? Why did *Notes* not instruct Christians to seek to understand how

Jews themselves define the State of Israel? Jews are left only to guess at answers to these questions. Consequently they have latched onto the most obvious proposition, that *Notes'* attitude must be in some way related to that Christian pseudo-theology which teaches about the rejection and dispossession of the Jews as being a punishment for their rejection of the Messiah.

The remote cause of the reactions is what Jewish leaders view as the unsatisfactory and discriminating nature of political arrangements between the Vatican and the State of Israel—that is to say, the fact that the Holy See has never established full de jure diplomatic relations with Israel.

However, the efficient and remote causes of the reactions are clearly connected in the minds of the Jewish commentators whose opinions were examined above. Jews do not distinguish them. For them, the statement in *Notes* is a confirmation of what they perceive to be the Catholic Church's rejection of Israel. Both the perceived efficient and remote causes of the reactions are signals for Jews of what they also interpret as the essential disregard in which the Catholic Church holds Jewish sensibilities about Israel.

Jewish reactions to the *Notes* are expressed through many accusations and allegations of a serious nature which represent Jewish points of view on the problem. However, further and closer investigation will begin to reveal yet another dimension to the problem.

III. The Problem of Antisemitism— and a Solution

Here we shall further clarify the nature of the problem caused by the existence of the State of Israel in the Catholic-Jewish dialogue by critically examining and responding to the relevant Jewish points of view: the many allegations and assertions made by Jewish leaders, noted in Chapter II. Thus we shall bring into sharper focus the nature of recognition for Israel which Jews seek from the Catholic Church, and then a different perspective on the nature of the problem in the dialogue will begin to emerge.

SUGGESTED CAUSES OF THE PROBLEM

Allegation 1: Jewish Punishment by Wandering and Homelessness

The pseudo-theology which holds that, because the Jews rejected the Christian Messiah, they are rejected by God and condemned forever to a punishment of homelessness, dispersion and wandering, is said by some Jews to be a fundamental reason for the Catholic Church's refusal to give full political and religious recognition to the State of Israel.[1] This opinion, as we have already observed in Chapter I, is also held by Charlotte Klein who claims that this pseudo-theology is residual in the Church's consciousness and is a major reason for her non-recognition of Israel.

This pseudo-theology was never defined as a binding Christian dogma, nor is it really proper to call it "doctrine" in the sense that it formed a part of the defined Magisterial teaching which has Apostolic origin. That it was a universally accepted aberrant Christian notion and that the Jews have suffered as a result of its perpetuation is unquestionable.[2] In the long history of Christianity this pseudo-theology has been present, and it has remained intact into the contemporary era.[3]

Christians should therefore not be surprised that some Jews believe that this aberrant notion is the rationale behind the Holy See's reluctance to give theological recognition to Israel. A glance at some official Catholic statements published over the past one hundred years finds the notion fully operative.

At the time of the first Zionist Congress in 1897 when the subject of the conjectured return of the Jews to Palestine was in the world news, the following statements were made by the Jesuit publication *Civiltà Cattolica:*

> 1,827 years have passed since the prediction of Jesus of Nazareth was fulfilled, namely, that Jerusalem would be destroyed . . . that the Jews would be led away to be slaves among all the nations and that they would remain in the dispersion until the end of the world.

> . . . according to the Sacred Scriptures the Jewish people must always live dispersed and vagabondo (vagrant) among the other nations so that they may render witness to Christ not only by the Scriptures . . . but by their very existence.

> As for a rebuilt Jerusalem which might become the center of a reconstructed State of Israel, we must add that this is contrary to the predictions of Christ himself who foretold that "Jerusalem would be downtrodden by the Gentiles until the time of the Gentiles is fulfilled" (Luke 21:24), that is . . . until the end of the world.[4]

The aberrant notion of the rejection and the eternal punishment of the Jews by dispossession is very clear here, and it is given as the reason why the Church could not accept a rebuilt "Jerusalem." And, furthermore, it is claimed that such recognition would be contrary to the predictions of Christ.

We find this idea expressed by Pius X in his reply to Theodor Herzl who pleaded with the Pope for a sympathetic understanding of the Zionist cause:

> We are unable to favour the movement. We cannot prevent the Jews from going to Jerusalem, but we could never sanction it. The ground of Jerusalem . . . has been sanctified by the life of Christ. As head of the Church I cannot answer you otherwise. The Jews have not recognized our Lord, therefore we cannot recognize the Jewish people.[5]

As an outcome of the audience Herzl recorded the Pope's answer in his diary in this manner:

> The Jewish faith was the foundation of our own, but it has been superseded by the teachings of Christ and we cannot admit that it still enjoys any validity.[6]

To Herzl the message was perfectly clear.

In 1922, at the news that Jewish settlers had allegedly evicted Arab proprietors from their land, *Civiltà Cattolica* commented:

> Jews have . . . forgotten that more than 1800 years have passed since their fathers smitten by divine malediction, or if this sounds unpleasant, subjugated by a hand stronger than theirs, were expelled and dispersed over the whole earth.[7]

Thus, according to this opinion, the Jews had committed a grave wrong in returning to Palestine.

In 1934 in a book defending the "Old Testament" as an integral part of the Christian revelation, Cardinal Faulhaber of Munich acknowledges only the Israel of the early biblical period:

> . . . after the death of Christ Israel was dismissed from the service of the Revelation. She had not known the time of her visitation. She had repudiated and rejected the Lord's Anointed, had driven him out of the City and had nailed him to the Cross. Then the veil of the Temple was rent, and with it the covenant between the Lord and his people. The daughter of Sion receives the bill of divorce, and from that time forth Assuerus wanders forever restless over the face of the earth.[8]

The pseudo-theology of dispossession as punishment is still alive in that great champion of the Jewish-Catholic dialogue and the main framer of *Nostra Aetate,* Cardinal Augustin Bea. In a section of his book *The Church and the Jewish People* entitled *"The Judgement Which Will Smite Jerusalem"* Bea writes:

> The fate of Jerusalem constitutes a sort of final reckoning at the end of a thousand years of infidelities and opposition to God. Here, too, it is not the fact of belonging to the people of Israel which determines the judgement but the act of opposing God and his prophets and messengers, above all Jesus . . . the judgement of Jerusalem and its destruc-

tion from part of God's revelation to man whereby he makes manifest in a particular episode something of the terrible reality of the judgement with which the story of mankind will end.[9]

Cardinal Bea is a perfect example of one whose heart, in regard to Jews and Judaism, was in the right place but whose head had not yet sufficiently emerged from the old supersessionist theology.

It can be seen in this evidence how well this pseudo-theology was entrenched in the Christian psyche. One cannot wonder that the same aberrant notion still dominates the contemporary Jewish mind in the face of the current problem of the Catholic Church and the recognition of the State of Israel.

That such a notion would simply cease to exist at any given time is not a very realistic expectation. Neither would one dare to assert that it no longer exists. It is, after all, the intellectual rationale which Christians gave to antisemitism.

Nevertheless, in the Magisterial teaching of the contemporary Catholic Church, the pseudo-theology of dispossession as punishment has been eradicated. Not only *Nostra Aetate*[10] but also the *Dogmatic Constitution on the Church* (*Lumen Gentium*) drew upon the strong affirmation of Paul in *The Letter to the Romans* (11:28–29) when seeking to define the role of the Jewish people in God's plan of salvation, even after the time of Christ:

> On account of their fathers, this people [*the Jews*] remains most dear to God, for God does not repent of the gifts He makes nor the calls He issues.[11]

The Jews, according to this statement, remain God's chosen people in the fullest sense. This affirmation is also found in the speeches, homilies and remarks of Pope John Paul II.

In Mainz the Pope addressed the Jewish community as "*the people of God of the Old Covenant which has never been revoked by God.*"[12] At another time he spoke of them as the people "*who have the adoption of sons and the glory of the covenants and the legislation and the worship and the promises.*"[13] Addressing the Anti-Defamation League of B'nai B'rith at another time the Pope said that "*the respect we speak of is based on the mysterious spiritual link which brings us close together, in Abraham, and through Abraham, in God who chose Israel and brought forth the Church from Israel.*"[14] Here is the antithesis of that pseudo-theology.

In a speech made in Australia the Pope's remarkable formulation distills years of theological development:

> The Catholic faith is rooted in the eternal truths of the Hebrew Scriptures and in the irrevocable covenant made with Abraham. We, too, gratefully hold these same truths of our Jewish heritage and look upon you as our brothers and sisters in the Lord.[15]

The arguments of Siegman, Hertzberg and Klein indicate that the reason why the Catholic Church refuses to recognize Israel formally is based on the lingering Christian pseudo-theology of Jewish rejection and punishment, implying that dispossession and wandering are rendered void in the light of this evidence from contemporary Catholic Magisterial teaching on the Jews.

Allegation 2: The Silence of the Holy See

Rabbi Meyer Jais and other Jewish critics and commentators speak about or allude to the silence of the Holy See.[16] A silence in response to requests for full de jure diplomatic arrangements. A silence in the face of danger to Israel. Such silence is interpreted by Jews to imply the Church's refusal to consider Jewish sensibilities about Israel and even the rejection of Israel itself. Thus it is seen as a cause of the problem.

Ruth and Nathan Perlmutter shed a more complete light upon this allegation. They write about the silence of the Catholic Church at the time when her Jewish partners in the dialogue needed her support most, during the Six Day War in 1967 and the Yom Kippur War in 1973. At these times the threat to Israel was the greatest it had ever been since 1948. Faced with this silence, they contend, Jews must ponder the real intentions of the Catholic Church, and they must reassess a relationship which has become very difficult to bear. The silence was not confined to these occasions only but was also maintained after the most outrageous statements and actions from Catholic officials. First, they cite, there is the Church's silence when the Secretary of State, Cardinal Cassaroli, met with Farouk Kaddoumi the Palestinian Liberation Organization's second-in-command to Yasser Arafat. Then again, when the Pope granted an audience to the Islamic Conference Organizations' secretary, Habib Chiatti, who later boasted that the Pope shared the same sentiments as the Arab world. Silence was the response to both the comment and the complaint that the Pope had met with a representative of an organization which had called for a Holy War with Israel. The Perlmutters also cite the case of the gun-running Archbishop Hilarion Cappucci who was supposed to have been inhibited by the Holy See and yet openly continues to propagandize on behalf of Arafat's terrorists. Why, the Perlmutters ask, has the Holy See chosen to be silent?

Immanuel Jakobovits, Chief Rabbi of the United Synagogue of Great Britain and Northern Ireland, also illuminates the meaning of the allegation of silence.[17] He deplores the *"screams of silence"* from Church leaders in the face of the massacres of Jews by Lebanese Christians. He contrasts the Church's outrage as a result of the Falangist Sabra and Chatila massacres. Why, he asks, the double standards? They betray for Jakobovits the depths of antisemitic prejudice that still lingers. Jewish statehood, concludes Jakobovits, has not solved the Jewish problem. It has not eliminated antisemitism and it has not made Jews equals among the nations. This failure is a hard disillusionment for Jews whose dreams for normalization of relationships with Catholics have been cruelly shattered by Israel's isolation and execration.

The reality of these facts of history is deplorable, and the silence of the Catholic Church in their presence is an unfathomable, inexplicable and embarrassing mystery belonging to the realm of the Holy See's internal political policy.[18]

In the presence of the accusations made against the Holy See's and Pius XII's silence during the period of the Holocaust, made notorious by Hochhuth's play,[19] Church silence has been invested with a sinister character. But is this true of the Catholic Magisterial silence on Israel?

Silence can be interpreted variously. In the cases of these cited historical instances it is impossible to guess just what it could mean without trivializing the very just complaints of Perlmutters and Jakobovits. In view of the non-recognition of the State of Israel, is it not conceivable that the Holy See's silence might indicate something other than refusal and rejection? Could it, in the light of *Notes* and remarks made in the homilies and speeches of Pope John Paul II, indicate cogitation and caution, given the characteristic conservative processes of the Holy See?

Jorge Mejia, Executive Secretary to the Holy See's Commission for Religious Relations with the Jews, reflects on the operation or method or, as he puts it, "style" of the Catholic Church:

> . . . changes . . . are never sudden. . . . They are the ripe fruit of first hidden currents, flowing below the surface, but well nourished by the fertile soil of authentic tradition. . . . Those aware of the changing

force of new ideas and insights know well that if they rush they only endanger their intuitions. They await the proper time, kairos, the time appointed by God's unfathomable design. Sometime an external fact or facts may serve as a catalytic factor, suddenly precipitating, as in chemistry, the hoped-for reaction. . . .[20]

Dr. Meir Mendes, a former Israeli Minister to the Holy See for thirteen years, shares Jorge Mejia's view of the Holy See's prudence. He stresses that *"the Vatican waited 60 years to recognize Italian rule over Rome."*[21] He argues that the Holy See, which is an extremely complex entity, never hurries but does change course at times. Mendes counsels against Jewish despair, claiming that it is altogether possible that the Holy See will one day give full de jure diplomatic recognition to Israel.

From those who have first-hand experience of the Holy See's processes it would appear that these silences should not be interpreted as refusals to recognize Israel but should be seen as the ordinary method of an extremely conservative and careful ecclesiastical administration. Nevertheless, it is an administration which, as we can detect through *Notes* and the remarks in the homilies and speeches of its leader Pope John Paul II,[22] is committed to serious reflection on the role of Israel for Jews, even though it is not yet fully equipped to speak on that subject.

Allegation 3: Political Motives

Among the imputed reasons for the Holy See's reticence to establish diplomatic ties with Israel are its concerns for Arab interests (Hertzberg),[23] and its reluctance to establish diplomatic ties with a nation with uncertain borders (*World Jewish Congress'* Commission on Interreligious Affairs).[24]

ARAB INTERESTS

"Arab interests" is a global and somewhat misleading statement. The only "Arab interests" which the Holy See has claimed are for peace in the Middle East (which has Israeli interests at heart too) and for the security of minority Christian and, more particularly, Arab-Christian groups in the Middle East.[25]

A number of the bishops of the Catholic Church are Arab, and so it is hardly likely that the Holy See would not have their pastoral concerns for their people at heart. There could be little doubt that one of the bishops' major concerns would be for what might happen to their people if the Holy See did give formal diplomatic recognition to Israel. It does not take a great stretch of the imagination to ponder what might transpire for Arab-Catholics and other Christians in such an event, given the current fundamentalist upsurge in the Arab States of the Middle East.

TERRITORIAL DISPUTES

The fact of Israel's frequently changing borders is a political reason given by the Holy See for not establishing formal diplomatic ties with Israel.[26]

John Oesterreicher has attempted to explain this reason. He argues that the Holy See cannot give recognition until there is some final settlement because to do so would be unjust to other parties,[27] specifically to Jordan, to Lebanon and to Egypt. Because the present political situation in the Middle East is so precarious, Oesterreicher contends, *"diplomatic recognition"* would be no more than a band-aid on a gaping wound and would solve none of the problems that beset Israel. Oesterreicher's solution to resolving the problem is that lovers of Zion should seek ways to bring understanding and reconciliation to Israel and her neighbors. This task, he claims, is the first priority of the Holy See as well.

Oesterreicher's explanation was fiercely attacked in a letter from *George Friedman* in the *New York Times*.[28] Friedman wrote that he did not know that the prerequisite for recognition from the Holy See was the creation of political Utopia, or that the Holy See confined diplomatic recognition to places where it could heal all wounds. Friedman pointed to the situation with El Salvador and Nicaragua and he asked why the Holy See appears to have one standard for Israel and another for other countries. Friedman concluded that the situation manifests the antisemitism which always has separate and unattainable standards for Jews. Other nations, he claimed, may be constantly at war, their economies a shambles and their people divided by ethnic strife, yet the Holy See has no problem establishing relations with them. Diplomatic approval, Friedman claimed, should merely be the first step in the Church's atonement for its historical crimes against the Jews.

Friedman's argument is strongly and understandably emotional but its weakness lies in the example which forms the basis of his argument. The political problems of El Salvador and Nicaragua are of an entirely different nature from Israel's problems. They are internal problems, matters of civil war. They are not territorial. They do not engage their immediate neighbors in border disputes.

Oesterreicher's explanation[29] for the Holy See's refusal to establish diplomatic ties with Israel while there exist questions of justice for other nations is at least reasonable. The position has its own logic and its own morality.

THE CITY OF JERUSALEM

Another reason advanced for the Holy See's refusal to establish relations with Israel is the disposition of the city of Jerusalem. Fundamentally it is a concern for the international and interfaith character of the city and also a concern for the Christian Holy Places. This subject has a long and well-documented history.[30] From time to time it is re-expressed, bringing forth weighty Jewish comment.[31] It is a concern which appears to remain and which is fueled by actions of fanatical fringe groups within Israeli Jewry.[32] However, there is evidence that since the unification of the city of Jerusalem in 1967 the Israeli Government has nurtured the interfaith character of that City.[33]

These three areas, the issue of Arab-Christians, the territorial rights of Israel's neighbors, and the interfaith character of the city of Jerusalem, remain concerns of the Holy See.

During the Gulf War (January–February 1991) a Declaration on Religious Relations Between the Holy See and the State of Israel was released by Dr. J. Navaro-Valls, Director of the Press Office of the Holy See. It appeared on January 25, 1991. The Declaration states that there *"have been or are specific and essential grounds why the Holy See does not have diplomatic relations,"* and that *"the reasons are not theological but juridical ones,"* and it proceeds to list them as (1) the still unresolved difficulties relating to Israel's presence in the Occupied Territories and her relationship with the Palestinians; (2) the annexation of the Holy City Jerusalem; and (3) the situation of the Catholic Church in Israel and in the territories administered by Israel.[34]

In practice there exist certain limited diplomatic relations between the Holy See and Israel. The Israeli embassy to Italy includes an officer, albeit now on a part-time basis, to the Vatican Secretariat of State. The Apostolic Delegate in Jerusalem communicates with the Israeli Ministry of Foreign Affairs. When Israeli leaders meet with the Pope, the protocol is that accorded to a state visit.[35] However, this partial, de facto recognition is not enough. The Jewish community wants full de jure formalization of the relationship. That is to say, it wants the Holy See to establish political relations with the State of Israel on the same basis as it has done with other nations by the mutual exchange of *full* diplomatic ties.

Eugene Fisher has asserted that de jure and de facto political recognition of Israel by the Holy See already exists unequivocally.[36] Fisher arrives at this conclusion from the Pope's statement concerning the State of Israel in *Redemptionis Anno* (1984). Here we find a very positive and affirmative statement about the State of Israel. Nevertheless, it does not amount to *full* de jure political recognition, and it is certain that the Jewish community, as evidenced in the reports in Chapter II, does not understand the Pope's statement as conferring full de jure recognition to the State of Israel.

Allegations 4 and 5: Conscious and Unconscious Antisemitism and Anti-Zionism

CATHOLIC UNCONSCIOUS ANTISEMITISM

On the one hand it has been said that the Catholic Church covers up its reluctance to recognize Israel by its loud denunciations of antisemitism (Hertzberg). Yet Friedman, on the other hand, has accused the Catholic Church of antisemitism because of its failure to recognize Israel officially. So the question emerges: Does the Catholic Church while denouncing antisemitism, practice antisemitism? Is this at the root of the problem in the dialogue?

The form of antisemitism in question is not that practiced by imputation but that practiced by the denial to recognize that Jews have the right of self-determining nationhood. The Catholic Church is seen to be practicing this form of antisemitism by its refusal to recognize Israel officially and the religious and ontological importance of the State for universal Jewry.

The allegation that non-recognition of Israel implies antisemitism is supported by a number of Christian scholars.

Jacques Maritain writes:

> To wish to reject into nothingness this return which finally was accorded to the Jewish people, and which permits it to have a shelter of its own in the world . . . is to wish that misfortune hound again this people, and that once more it be the victim of iniquitous aggression. Anti-Israelism is no better than antisemitism.[37]

Edward Flannery contends that anti-Zionism is a repository of unconscious antisemitism.[38] Anti-Zionism, he argues, began in full force after the Six Day War in 1967. Before that time, it was relatively anemic. Flannery argues that this new form of antisemitism came in the form of sympathy for the Arab refugees and for Arab national aspirations: all third world ideologies. So, as antisemitism appears to disappear, anti-Zionism takes its place. It is, Flannery asserts, a unifier of Arabs and Communists, Protestants and Catholics, leftists and rightists, blacks and whites, thus demonstrating the same character as the age-old antisemitism. Its core rests on two fallacies. First, the fallacy of defining Judaism as *only* a religion, not as a peoplehood and nation which it is essentially. Second, the fallacy of the refusal to allow Jews to define themselves because then it would be seen that throughout their history Jews have defined themselves as a people wedded to a land, a homeland, Israel, and to a religion.

Flannery notices degrees of anti-Zionism. The first degree has a genocidal intent to destroy Israel, and it is to be found among some Arabs and some Soviets, as in other extremists. This is its conscious manifestation. The second degree is *unconscious,* and is to be found in the silence of the churches in the face of danger to Israel's existence.

In a strongly argued paper the Protestant theologian *Roy Eckardt* denounces the pernicious persistence of antisemitism which exists, he perceives, "*just under the surface*" of Christianity.[39] It is seen by the fact that Jews are forever on trial, that they are always the subjects of investigations, evaluations and judgments. He asserts that "*Christian antisemitism is nowhere more alive and well than in Christian anti-Israelism.*"

Does antisemitism lurk residually, unconsciously, in the Catholic Church's refusal to establish full de jure diplomatic ties with Israel? Is it inherent in the statement concerning Israel in the *Notes?* Is the Catholic Church anti-Zionist? These are questions prompted by the allegations and inferences in Maritain's, Flannery's and Eckardt's writings.

All of these writers speak about "antisemitism" as an expression used for "Jew-hatred." Flannery identifies what he expresses as an *unconscious* antisemitism in the Church. Eckardt writes about an antisemitism in Christianity—and thus by implication within the Catholic Church— which is "*just under the surface*": another way of expressing "unconscious" antisemitism.

Is *unconscious* antisemitism a possibility? To hate is an expression of consciousness. Hatred is a state which can only exist in consciousness. Without consciousness there can be no act of hating. To speak about an "unconscious" hatred is therefore illogical. Thus, to speak of "unconscious" Jew-hatred is also illogical. This is not to deny that *antisemitisms* still reside deeply in Christian and, in particular, Catholic unconsciousness. They are the inheritance of a continuing European cultural antisemitism which, as we have seen above, was nurtured for two thousand years on Christian teaching and attitudes concerning the Jews, and they appear from time to time like "freudian slips."[40]

CATHOLIC ANTISEMITISM

Maritain, Flannery and Eckardt have argued that *anti-Zionism* is an expression of antisemitism. Can it be held that the Catholic Church by withholding full political relations with the State of Israel is essentially anti-Zionist and antisemitic?

In her official teaching the Church has the following to say about Jew-hatred or "antisemitism":

[*The Church*] deplores the hatred, persecutions, and displays of anti-semitism directed against the Jews at any time and from any source.[41]

. . . we may simply restate here that the spiritual bonds and historical links binding the Church to Judaism condemn (as opposed to the very spirit of Christianity) all forms of antisemitism and discrimination, which in any case the dignity of the human person alone would suffice to condemn.[42]

Education and catechesis should concern themselves with the problem of racism, still active in different forms of antisemitism (*there follows a reiteration of the teaching about antisemitism from* Nostra Aetate *and from* Guidelines). That is what these notes aim to remedy. This would mean that the Council text and "Guidelines and Suggestions" would be more easily and ever faithfully put into practice.[43]

The abhorrence of antisemitism is a major theme which runs through many of the homilies and addresses of Pope John Paul II. In his very first audience with Jewish representatives the Pope reaffirmed the Second Vatican Council's repudiation of antisemitism "*as opposed to the very spirit of Christianity . . . which in any case the dignity of the human person alone would suffice to condemn.*"[44] The Pope has repeated this message in all countries he has visited. On the twentieth anniversary of *Nostra Aetate* he stated that "*antisemitism in its ugly and sometimes violent manifestations should be completely eradicated.*"[45]

The Pope's address to Jewish leaders at Miami in the United States of America in September 1987[46] is absolutely clear in its condemnation of antisemitism and of its fruits in the "*satanic method*" of the Nazi Holocaust. In this address Pope John Paul II recalls the "*strong unequivocal efforts of the Popes* (his predecessors Pius XI and Pius XII) *against antisemitism and Nazism at the height of the persecution against the Jews."* He stresses his deep sense of revulsion against the cruel indignities heaped upon the Jews in conquered countries.

The strongest Magisterial statement to date condemning antisemitism was issued by the Pontifical Committee "Justitia et Pax" in which the following is expressed:

> Amongst the manifestations of systematic racial distrust, specific mention must once again be made of anti-semitism. If anti-semitism has been the most tragic form that racist ideology has assumed in our century, with the horrors of the Jewish "holocaust," it has unfortunately not yet entirely disappeared. . . . Terrorist acts which have Jewish persons or symbols as their target have multiplied in recent years and show the radicalism of such groups. . . . In order firmly to reject such actions, and eradicate racist behavior of all sorts from our societies as well as the mentalities that lead to it, we must hold strongly to convictions about the dignity of every human person and the unity of the human race. Morality flows from these convictions.[47]

It is in Pope John Paul II's speech to the Jewish community of Australia in Sydney on November 26, 1986 that we find the most absolute condemnation of antisemitism. On that occasion the Pope announced that antisemitism *"must be held to be sinful."*[48] Nothing more damnable could be said of antisemitism than to equate it with sin.

In these statements from the official teaching of the Catholic Church is irrefutable evidence of the Catholic Church's vehement and absolute repudiation of antisemitism.

It cannot be denied that antisemitism, Jew-hatred, is a shameful part of the Church's history right down to the present era. This is a fact which cannot be reversed. It is a possibility that antisemitism and shades of antisemitism still lurk in the minds of some Catholics since the educational processes have still a long way to reach. However, in the light of the evidence contained in the Magisterial teaching it cannot be reasonably held that antisemitism is part of the official teaching of the Catholic Church or that it is a motivating force in any of her actions or affairs with Jews, no matter how mistaken or ill-informed or unpopular it might be.

CATHOLIC ANTI-ZIONISM

Anti-Zionism is that force which operates against Zionism[49] with the intention to prevent the Jewish people from attaining the fullness of their Jewishness by their return to the land of God's promise.[50]

Can anti-Zionism be claimed to be the intention of the Catholic Church or the fundamental motive for her silence, reticence, caution, reserve vis-à-vis Israel?

In the perspective of history surveyed earlier this allegation would certainly be valid. In the statements of Pius X and of *Civiltà Cattolica* we see very clear anti-Zionist sentiments expressed and a quasi-theological basis is provided for them. The question, however, is a contemporary one and, reframed for the present-day Catholic Church, asks whether current Magisterial teaching is anti-Zionist.

A fundamental proposition of anti-Zionism is the denial of the historical continuity of Israel since 70 CE.[51] However, *Notes* very clearly recognizes the following in regard to Israel:

(1) the Jewish attachment to *"the land of their forefathers"* with its biblical roots;

(2) the existence of the State of Israel;

(3) Israel's right to exist under the common principles of international law in the same way that other states have a place in the community of nations.

The Catholic Church clearly recognizes the historical continuity between Israel at 70 CE and Israel today:

> The history of Israel did not end in 70 AD. . . .[52] It continued, especially in a numerous Diaspora which allowed Israel to carry to the whole world a witness . . . while preserving the memory of the land of their forefathers at the heart of their hope (*Passover Seder*).[53]

The Holy See recognizes that:

> The permanence of Israel (while so many ancient peoples have disappeared without trace) is an historic fact and a sign to be interpreted within God's design.[54]

These statements are clearly affirmative of Jewish sensibilities toward the land and of the State of Israel itself. Even though they fall short of Jewish expectation, the statements are clear and unambiguous evidence that the Catholic Church is not in intent anti-Zionist.

Clearly, in the face of this evidence it cannot be reasonably maintained that anti-Zionism is the fundamental reason for Catholic nonformal recognition of Israel.

Most Allegations Are Without Substance

Thus far the investigation in this chapter has addressed allegations and assertions which appeared to many Jewish and some Christian commentators on Catholic-Jewish dialogue to be related to or the cause of the problem of Israel in the dialogue. We have found that many of these have their roots in the history of relationships between Jews and Catholics, but that in the new chapter of Jewish-Catholic relations which began with the Second Vatican Council these allegations and assertions are without substance in reality, even though they appear to be, understandably, deeply embedded in Jewish memory. We have also found that other assertions of a political nature are purely speculative and often illinformed.

A NEW FACTOR: JEWISH INSECURITY REVEALED

From many of the Jewish voices in Chapter II we can detect a strong, visceral sense of insecurity related to the future of the State of Israel. It has been asserted that if the Holy See would enter into full de jure diplomatic relations with Israel, then this would effectively remove any notion of the impermanence of Israel's existence in the minds of her enemies. It would also be the decisive step toward the establishment of peace in the Middle East. This is raised as a matter of great urgency in the letter of the World Jewish Congress.

The urgency with which the World Jewish Congress' letter is marked is doubtlessly motivated by the fact that ever since November 29, 1947, when the United Nations determined to acknowledge the Jewish claim to their homeland in Palestine, Arab states have subverted the intention of the United Nations. Since 1948 they have sought the destruction of the State of Israel. This was an announced plan, accompanied by many Arab leaders' promises to wreak genocide on the Jews living in Israel.[55]

The seriousness with which the Holy See's perceived de facto position is held by Jews can be gauged by the fact that on January 5, 1988 the State of Israel changed its liaison with the Holy See from a full-time to a part-time position. This move was seen by an unnamed official in Rome as a diplomatic expression of displeasure at the current state of relations between the Holy See and Israel. Theodore Freedman, director of the European office of the Anti-Defamation League of B'nai B'rith, is reported to have said that the move communicates some dissatisfaction on the part of Israel, a way of indicating that Israel is not happy with the limited de facto relationship.[56]

In this political action we can detect the degree to which the Holy See's position in withholding full de jure diplomatic relations with Israel has irritated Jewish people. It is certainly a statement which speaks more loudly than the words of the many critics and commentators whose opinions were reported in Chapter II. It also demonstrates how viscerally basic Israel is to contemporary Jews.

Lightly camouflaged beneath these assertions and allegations is a deep-seated Jewish insecurity associated with the safety and continued existence of the State of Israel. The several Jewish spokespeople plead for Israel as they would plead for their own existence. The assertions and allegations are instruments of their pleading.

WHAT IS THE NATURE OF THE RECOGNITION SOUGHT BY JEWS FOR ISRAEL?

The real nature of the problem of Israel in the Catholic-Jewish dialogue is more clearly revealed by an examination of the demands for recognition which come from the Jewish world community.

A Threefold Recognition

The evidence adduced in Chapter II and thus far in this chapter indicates that Jewish recognition sought for Israel falls into three categories.

Some Jews ask simply for *political recognition.* This means that the Holy See should formalize its existing de facto relationship with Israel by establishing full de jure diplomatic ties with that nation. Recognition by the *common principles of international law* as suggested in *Notes* is not sufficient.

Some want Israel recognized at the political level but also they want Israel recognized as a central reality for universal Jewish existence, secular and/or religious. These Jews seek *political and ontological recognition.*

Other Jews seeking political and ontological recognition for Israel also want religious recognition. This group is unhappy that *Notes* recommends against religious interpretations. These Jews seek *political, ontological and religious recognition* for Israel.

A Threefold Challenge

Together these sought-for recognitions constitute a threefold challenge to the Catholic Church.

THE POLITICAL CHALLENGE

The de facto diplomatic relations which exist between the Holy See and the State of Israel, even though they are not of the nature which Jews would have them, are evidence that the Holy See already gives political recognition to Israel. Nevertheless, it is apparent from the strength and urgency of the emotional criticisms and requests that Jews want a political recognition beyond that which already exists. They want the establishment of political arrangements on the same basis as those which the Holy See has established with other nations, and they anxiously await the Holy See's response.

THE ONTOLOGICAL CHALLENGE

This challenge has already been partly met by the Catholic Church, and *Notes* expresses it in the following way:

> The history of Israel did not end in 70 AD. . . . It continued, especially in a numerous Diaspora . . . while preserving the memory of the land of their forefathers at the heart of their hope.[57]

This teaching is reiterated in *Redemptionis Anno* where Pope John Paul II makes reference to Israel in the following way:

> For the Jewish people who live in the State of Israel and who preserve in that land such precious testimonies of their history and their faith, we must ask for the desired security and the due tranquility that is the prerogative of every nation and condition of life and of progress for every society.[58]

However, there is still a problem for Jews in this statement since it implies ontological recognition of Israel as important for Israeli Jews but not, as is demanded, for *all* Jews everywhere.

THE THEOLOGICAL CHALLENGE

The demand for religious (for Catholics, more appropriately termed "theological") recognition from the majority of Jewish commentators reported in Chapter II is clear and strong. Nevertheless, most of the commentators who press for theological recognition of Israel do not indicate the nature of the recognition which they seek. Waxman speaks about the profound religious significance which the restoration of Israel has in terms of the confirmation of the covenant with the land and mentions "implications" without further specification. Toaff is more explicit in telling us that the return signals the coming of the final redemption of the whole human race, and also Israel's role in that event. These two suggestions of what might be involved in theological recognition, vague though they are, indicate theological issues which are not immediately apparent on the theological agenda of the Catholic Church.

In the reports in Chapter II it is clear that Jews want Christians to recognize and to understand them in the reality of their contemporary existence. The Catholic Church, they contend, ought to concern itself with the reality of how Jews are at the end of the twentieth century CE and in the light of the momentous events of the Holocaust and the rebirth of the Jewish nation in the State of Israel. Any theological recognition ought to reflect the reality of contemporary Jewish existence. Recognition ought not to be based on the notions and categories of biblical theology, nor upon ways in which Jews have been or are seen in the minds of theologians. Such interpretations reduce Jews to the realm of ideas.

It is precisely the latter which makes the statement about the land in *Notes* so totally unpalatable to Jews. The *Notes* recommend that Christians understand the Jewish attachment to the land as a *"religious attachment which finds its roots in biblical tradition."*[59] This means, as a *religious* notion, biblically based. The authors appear to back away from the *contemporary reality* by suggesting that Christians do not make their own *"any particular religious interpretation"* of the biblical tradition and the State of Israel, and, furthermore, the authors recommend that the State of Israel and its political options *"should be envisaged not in a perspective which is in itself religious. . . ."* In the Jewish view this method for recognizing the State of Israel stands in stark opposition to the terms of recognition sought.

By the same token, the designation *"Religious"* in the title of the Holy See's *Commission for Religious Relations with the Jews* is also inappropriate since it implies either that Jews are exclusively a religious community which they are not, since they clearly regard themselves as *a people*,[60] or that the Catholic Church is only concerned with Judaism as a religious phenomenon, and that nothing outside that narrow view of Judaism matters to the Catholic Church.

It would therefore seem appropriate that any response to the Jewish theological challenge by the Catholic Church should be concerned that theological recognition should not be a recognition of theological notions but should be a theological recognition of the contemporary reality of Jewish national identity and of its centrality for contemporary Jewish existence.

The Essence of the Recognition Sought by Jews for Israel

These demands for recognition reveal that world-Jewry pleads for a recognition of Israel which is intrinsic to Jewish existence, not merely an extrinsic notional political/religious recognition.

NEW DIMENSIONS OF THE PROBLEM EMERGE

Thus it can be seen that the problem of Israel in the Catholic-Jewish dialogue is beginning to reveal new dimensions. The various allegations and assertions and the threefold challenge for recognition of Israel now appear to veil a fundamental Jewish existential insecurity.

Throughout the reports in Chapter II Jewish commentators implicitly and explicitly associate Catholic recognition of the State of Israel with its safety and continuing security. In their minds Israel's safety and security is inextricably linked with the well-being of contemporary universal Jewish existence. Recognition of Israel is seen by them as an affirmation of contemporary Jewish existence. By the same token non-recognition of the State of Israel or even the slightest negativity relating to it is experienced as a blow to contemporary Jewish existence.

It is therefore apparent that a major factor of the problem of Israel in the Catholic-Jewish dialogue is that the statement concerning Israel in *Notes,* with the present state of diplomatic relations between Israel and the Holy See, does not satisfy contemporary Jewish existential needs but, on the contrary, contributes to an abiding and deeply felt contemporary Jewish insecurity.

Non-Jews will only come to understand this Jewish reaction to perceived Catholic attitudes within the perspective of Jewish experience which distinguishes Jews from all other peoples. The first is the experience of almost two thousand years of dispossession of their homeland which reduced them to wanderers, strangers and guests at the sufferance of their host countries. This was an existence of seeking survival, and that against all odds, the greatest of which was antisemitism which led to the Holocaust. The second experience has occurred since the creation of the State of Israel in 1948. Since that event there has never been a time when the existence of the Jewish State, which, as we have seen, is inextricably linked in the Jewish mind with continuing Jewish existence, has not been the subject of questioning and threat, not only from the Arab world but also from significant sectors of the Western world. Since the Israeli wars of 1967 and 1973 Jews have experienced a growth in hostility to Israel and its supporters. Increasingly, extreme left-wing sources throughout the world have attacked Israel's right to exist.[61]

One Jewish writer expresses the situation in these terms:

> While the Jewish people and religion were able to survive almost 1900 years in exile, without a state of their own, the loss of Israel today, so soon after the Holocaust, would be a trauma from which the entire people might never recover. Any religious group that could not recognize the right of Jews to sovereignty over one tiny portion of the earth's surface, or support the threatened state when Egyptian armies mobilized on its borders and tried to sever its economic jugular vein at Sharm al Sheikh, or when Egypt and Syria initiated a massive surprise attack on Yom Kippur, did not seem to be an appropriate partner for authentic dialogue. If you hestitate and waver over my brother's right to survive, what is there to discuss?[62]

For the problem in the dialogue to shift toward resolution, it is vital that Jewish existential insecurity relating to Israel, such as has been revealed here, be recognized by the Catholic partner in the dialogue and responded to with appropriate affirmative action.

QUESTIONS AND DIRECTIONS FOR REFOCUSING THE PROBLEM IN THE DIALOGUE

Several questions emerge from the investigation in this chapter.

- Why is the statement concerning the State of Israel in *Notes* expressed in the way it is?

- Is the statement about Israel in *Notes* a flat dismissal of religious recognition of Israel and thereby a dismissal of the sensibilities of Jews toward Israel?

- Does the Catholic Church have an *"evolving attitude"* to Israel, as Eugene Fisher suggests?

- Is the Jewish view of the problem in the dialogue too closely focused on the official Catholic teaching in the statement in *Notes* and therefore needing to be directed to the broader view?

- Are the theological views on the significance of Israel in Waxman's and Toaff's statements typical Jewish views or are there other views to be considered?

- Does the general vagueness of Jewish opinions on the religious significance of the return of Jews to the land and the rebirth of the nation-State of Israel in the reports in Chapter II suggest that Jewish theology has not fully matured on this subject, that it is still evolving?

- Is the Catholic Church able to accept the Jewish theological challenge which seeks theological recognition for Israel and the events surrounding its rebirth?

These questions suggest the further areas for investigation. First, an examination of the Catholic Magisterial teaching on Israel and on its attitudes toward Jewish sensibilities to Israel. Second, an investigation of imputedly difficult theological propositions which are said to prevent Catholic theological recognition of Israel. Thereafter an investigation of the interpretation of Israel by Jews.

IV. Official Catholic Teaching and the State of Israel

In this chapter we shall critically investigate and assess Catholic Magisterial teaching for its attitudes to Israel and to Jewish sensibilities about Israel. This will cover the following official Catholic teachings:

The *Declaration on the Relationship of the Church to Non-Christian Religions* (October 28, 1965),[1] commonly and hereafter, referred to as *Nostra Aetate,* which is the ordinary Magisterial teaching of the Second Vatican Council.[2]

Guidelines and Suggestions for Implementing the Conciliar Document "Nostra Aetate" (*no 4*) (December 1, 1974), referred to popularly and herein as *Guidelines* (*1974*), or sometimes as the *Vatican Guidelines.* This document was published over the signature of Cardinal Willebrands in his capacity as President of the then-newly-created Commission for the Catholic Church's Religious Relations with the Jews. The document is technically a directory.[3] It is derivative from *Nostra Aetate,* as its full title implies, and it both draws upon and amplifies its teaching.[4] *Guidelines* (*1974*) contains the ordinary Magisterial teaching of the Church.

Notes on the Correct Way To Present the Jews and Judaism in Preaching and Catechesis in the Roman Catholic Church (June 24, 1985), commonly and herein referred to as *Notes.* This document also promotes and extends the teaching of *Nostra Aetate* and, in particular, it takes up the theme of *Guidelines* (*1974*), Chapter III, *Teaching and Education,* which presupposes the thorough formation of instructors and educators in primary schools, seminaries and universities.[5] *Notes* also contains the ordinary Magisterial teaching of the Church.

The homilies and addresses of Pope John Paul II directed to specific Jewish groups on differing occasions. These also contain the ordinary Magisterial teaching of the Catholic Church.

Guidelines issued by regional bishops' conferences and by particular churches, hereafter referred to as *Episcopal Guidelines*, all of which are directives to particular churches. These documents also have the status of ordinary Magisterial teaching.[6] Their function is pastoral, having the intention to promote and facilitate the teaching of *Nostra Aetate, Guidelines (1974)* and *Notes* at the particular and local Church levels.

THE STATE OF ISRAEL: NOSTRA AETATE, GUIDELINES (1974), AND NOTES

The State of Israel is not mentioned in *Nostra Aetate* nor in *Guidelines (1974)*, and first comes into view, as we have already observed, in *Notes*.

The total silence in *Nostra Aetate* and *Guidelines (1974)* provokes the following questions:

- Did the framers of *Nostra Aetate* choose to ignore the issue of Israel or was this an innocent omission?

- Were the authors of *Nostra Aetate* aware of the religious significance which the State of Israel holds for many Jewish people?

- Why was there no reference made to the State of Israel nine years later in the *Guidelines (1974)*?

- Why did it take twenty years for the Holy See to mention the State of Israel and its meaning for Jews in the *Notes* of 1985?

- Why is *Notes* cautious about religious interpretations of Israel?

These questions will be pursued in the following section in which concerns with the development of these three documents will be discussed.

THE DEVELOPMENT OF NOSTRA AETATE AND THE DOCUMENTS OF THE HOLY SEE

Nostra Aetate

Of particular relevance to this study is the nature of the opposition which the framers of *Nostra Aetate* met throughout its passage at the

Second Vatican Council and the subsequent measures which they took to defend the document.

ARAB OPPOSITION

From the earliest days of the Council the "Jewish document," as the precursor to paragraph IV of *Nostra Aetate* was called,[7] found tough opposition from a group of Middle Eastern prelates[8] who feared that it would be misunderstood in their own Arab lands as a gesture in favor of the State of Israel.[9]

THE "JEWISH DOCUMENT" AND NOSTRA AETATE

Years before the definitive voting and after much argumentation with the committee responsible for the "Jewish Document," its authors decided,[10] in order to counteract any political accusations, to insert this document in the widest possible context of the attitude of the Catholic Church to non-Christian religions in general.[11] Thus the "Jewish Document" became the fourth paragraph of the *Declaration on the Relationship of the Church to Non-Christian Religions.*[12]

MOUNTING ANTISEMITISM

Yet even this maneuver did not solve the problem. "Holy war" broke out against the Decree.[13] In the Middle East demonstrations took place; there was even the threat of schism. In Rome numerous pamphlets were distributed warning about Zionist infiltration at the heart of the Church. It was objected that if the Decree were accepted the Church would have to suffer reprisals in Arab countries.[14]

CARDINAL BEA STEERS THE DOCUMENT AWAY FROM POLITICAL ASSOCIATIONS

Because of these increasing political difficulties Cardinal Bea, Secretary of the Secretariat for Christian Unity, which was responsible for the progress of the Declaration, made every effort to steer the text on the Jews and Judaism, now set in the Declaration, away from any sort of political interpretation or implication. He wanted to emphasize its purely religious nature and concerns. Such efforts are to be seen in Bea's November 1963 *Address to the Council Fathers*[15] where he tries to persuade them that there was no question of the Holy See giving recognition to the State of Israel.

> Before all else let us say what we are not talking about. There is no national or political question here. In particular, there is no question

of recognition of the State of Israel by the Holy See. None of such questions are dealt with or even touched upon. The schema treats exclusively of a purely religious question.

Bea concludes the Address:

> Lastly: since we are here treating a merely religious question, there is obviously no danger that the Council will get entangled in those difficult questions regarding the relations between the Arab nations and the State of Israel, or regarding so-called Zionism.[16]

Similar assurances were given at another Address to the Council in October 1964:

> As regards the Jewish people, it must again and again be made clear that the question is in no sense political, but is purely religious. We are not talking about Zionism, or the political State of Israel, but about the followers of the Mosaic religion, wherever in the world they may dwell.

And again in October 1965 Bea stressed:

> All efforts have aimed . . . to assure the clear expression of the exclusively religious nature of the schema, so as to close off any opening to political interpretation.[17]

THE PROMULGATION OF THE DECLARATION ON THE RELATIONSHIP OF THE CHURCH TO NON-CHRISTIAN RELIGIONS

Because of these prudent procedures the Declaration arrived at a happy conclusion. It was accepted with only 88 dissenting votes out of 2,300.[18] Thereafter the promulgation of the Declaration proceeded without difficulty.[19] It was the first time in history that the Church had proposed fraternal dialogue with the great non-Christian religions.

Political and Practical Reasons Prevail

THE DELIBERATE OMISSION OF ISRAEL

It is apparent from the primary sources cited above that any reference to the State of Israel was deliberately avoided by the framers of *Nostra Aetate* for political and practical reasons. The political reason was linked to the Church's Arab presence in the Middle East; the practical reason was the survival of the document itself.[20]

CARDINAL BEA AND THE STATE OF ISRAEL

In Bea's speeches we note how he distinguished the State of Israel as a purely political entity.[21] He seemed to have no idea of its religious significance for most Jews. He believed that the Declaration treated Judaism or, as he called it, the *"Mosaic religion,"* as an entirely religious phenomenon . . . *"the schema treats exclusively of a purely religious question" "we are treating a merely religious question"*; *"the question is . . . purely religious . . . exclusively religious."* For Bea, and thus for the Declaration, the return of Jews to their ancient homeland and the rebirth of the Jewish nation in the State of Israel held no religious significance. It was a totally political phenomenon.

The same can be said of Bea's attitude to Zionism. He saw this as an exclusively political movement. He spoke about it as *"so-called Zionism."* Bea linked Zionism with *"the political state of Israel."* There was no suggestion of its being a religious movement as well as a political force.

IGNORANCE OF JEWISH RELIGIOUS VIEWS OF ZIONISM

From Bea's statements there emerges what appears to be an ignorance of any idea that Zionism and the State of Israel were laden with religious significance for most Jews.

Evidence of this naiveté toward the religious significance of Zionism and the State of Israel for Jews is also to be found in the record of the entire debate as it is presented by J. Oesterreicher in 1968.[22] In this account the approach to Jews and Judaism is a purely theological one. Wherever Zionism or the State of Israel is raised it is always as a political issue and never in any way with religious overtones. There is a total absence in this work of any idea that Zionism or the State of Israel has any religious significance whatever for Jews.[23]

NOSTRA AETATE REFLECTS THE IGNORANCE OF ITS FRAMERS

The ignorance of those involved in framing the document has obviously spilled over into the document *Nostra Aetate* itself. This, along with the avoidance of any political troubles, would explain the document's silence on the State of Israel.

NOSTRA AETATE—NOT A DEFINITIVE STATEMENT

The nature of the Council's Declaration is also to be taken into consideration in assessing *Nostra Aetate*'s omission of Israel. Declarations were prepared by the Council Fathers to present teaching that was evolving and which had not yet reached a definitive stage.[24] Thus it can be argued that *Nostra Aetate* was never meant to be the final word on Jews and Judaism and, by implication, that its silence on Israel was not meant to be interpreted as a definitive statement.

Guidelines (1974)

Guidelines (1974) is technically a directory,[25] the function of which is to provide basic principles of pastoral theology taken from the Magisterium of the Church and especially from the Second Vatican Council. Directories are more particularly addressed to Bishops to give them assistance in practical matters.[26]

We have also noted that Israel was not mentioned in *Guidelines (1974)* and that its emphasis was on teaching and education: the practical concern to implement the teaching of *Nostra Aetate* in Catholic schools and Institutes of learning and higher education.

Notes

Eleven years later in 1985 and through the initiative of Pope John Paul II,[27] *Guidelines (1974)* was followed by *Notes*. This document is also technically a directory. Monsignor, now Bishop, Jorge Mejia, Secretary for the Commission for Religious Relations with Jews, informs us that the idea of *Notes*

> was to be of help to those engaged in catechetical work, in teaching and also in preaching, and to put into practice the new directions (of *Guidelines 1974*) . . . which are not always easy to translate into teaching methods,

and that

> it is intended to provide a helpful frame of reference for those who are called upon in various ways in the course of their teaching assignments to speak about Jews and Judaism, and who wish to do so in keeping with the current teaching of the Church in this area.[28]

Mejia goes on to explain that *Notes* seeks to promote the formation of Catholics for objectivity, justice and tolerance and especially for understanding dialogue.

NOSTRA AETATE, GUIDELINES, NOTES, AND THE THEOLOGICAL RECOGNITION OF ISRAEL

The nature of theological recognition sought for Israel, which was identified above, stresses that it *"should not be a recognition of theological notions, but a theological recognition of the contemporary reality of Jewish national identity, and of its centrality for contemporary Jewish being,"* that is to say, that it should be concerned with how Jews are today in the light of Jewish return to the land of Israel and the rebirth of the Jewish nation in the State of Israel. *Nostra Aetate* does not measure up to this requirement since it is totally concerned with biblical and theological notions relating to Israel of the past, and with issues of the past, even though they might be vital for the future. The document treats Judaism as a theological phenomenon rather than as a contemporary reality in the world. Its saving feature in this regard is that it exhorts Catholics to have an attitude of friendship and openness to Jews.[29]

Both *Guidelines* (*1974*) and *Notes* continue to deal with Judaism as a theological phenomenon related to Christianity, and with the various biblical and theological notions which surround Judaism. However, *Notes* begins to move away from this treatment of Judaism to seeing it as a contemporary reality with a life of its own. We see evidences of this in Section VI which treats of *Judaism and Christianity in History* and which includes statements about

- *the permanence of Israel;*

- *the State of Israel;*

- *the Holocaust.*[30]

As slight as these references are, they are evidence of the Catholic Magisterium beginning to be aware of Judaism as a contemporary reality in its own right, with an independent life and purpose, and not just as the religious phenomenon from which Christianity has derived. This is a significant development since the time of the Second Vatican Council whose Fathers viewed Jews and Judaism primarily in their relationship to Christian origins. It is an advancement toward the criteria for theological recognition noted above.

Nevertheless, when *Notes* touches on the religious significance of the State of Israel it does a *volte face,* recommending that Christians regard the creation of the State of Israel in the terms of biblical tradition but not by any contemporary religious interpretations.[31] In this way the authors of *Notes* demonstrate that they are not prepared to cede a theological recognition to Israel as an expression of the contemporary reality of Jewish being, but only to a theological notion: *"the religious attachment which finds its roots in Biblical tradition."*

Eugene Fisher has explained *Notes'* caveat about the religious interpretation of the State of Israel in terms of its codicil (*cf. Declaration of the U.S. Conference of Catholic Bishops, November 20, 1975*). In that document we find the following statement:

> In dialogue with Christians, Jews have explained that they do not consider themselves a church, a sect, or a denomination, as is the case among Christian communities, but rather as a peoplehood that is not solely racial, ethnic or religious, but in a sense a composite of all these. It is for such reasons that an overwhelming majority of Jews see themselves bound in one way or another to the land of Israel. Most Jews see this tie to the land as essential to their Jewishness. Whatever difficulties Christians may experience in sharing this view, they should strive to understand this link between the land and people which Jews have expressed in their writings and worship throughout two millennia as a longing for the homeland, holy Zion. Appreciation of this link is not to give assent *to any particular religious interpretation (emphasis added)* of this bond. Nor is this affirmation meant to deny the legitimate rights of other parties in the region.[32]

Fisher argues that both caveats, the one in the U.S. Bishops' Statement and the other in *Notes,* are warnings against biblical fundamentalism which attempts to determine the boundaries of the modern state by reference to this or that biblical passage.[33] Furthermore Fisher claims[34] that the caveats in both documents have in mind views of biblical promises espoused by the Reverend Jerry Falwell and the late Rabbi Meir Kahane, one a Christian, and the other a Jewish, fundamentalist. Fisher argues that *Notes* does not intend to qualify the validity of the "bond" between people and land, but

> given the wide range of views within Judaism regarding its nature and implications even today, reflects that the Holy See is not quite ready to hazard a final judgement on those complex questions. Further dialogue with Jews and internal theological reflection within the Church on the results of that dialogue are clearly necessary.

Fisher might well be right about *Notes'* intention. His explanation is eminently reasonable. Nevertheless, the problem remains for the Jewish reader who does not have the benefit of Fisher's commentary. Even if the Jewish reader were to inquire of the U.S. Bishops' Statement to which the codicil in *Notes* refers, that reader would still be faced with ambiguity because there is nothing in that document which would enlighten the Jewish reader about biblical fundamentalist interpretations adhering to the State of Israel and its borders. Thus a prima facie interpretation of the statement in *Notes* is all that is left to the Jewish reader. This is a major deficiency in the document which needs to be taken into careful consideration in view of the problem arising from the document's statement concerning Israel at VI, 25.

Guidelines and Notes—Not Theological Treatises

There is a tendency, mostly implicit, by some of the critics of *Guidelines* (*1974*) and *Notes,* both Jewish and Christian, to expect a more fully developed doctrine on Jews and Judaism from these documents, as though they were theological treatises.[35] However, as we have noted already, these documents are of a very practical nature, and of necessity they leave much unsaid and unfinished. Both documents give the impression that there is more to come than is to be found within their contents. Indeed, we have observed how *Notes* took up the theme of Chapter III in *Guidelines* (*1974*) on *Teaching and Education,* which was only barely touched on in *Guidelines* (*1974*) but more fully elaborated by *Notes* nine years later. Presumably this pattern may recur in the future by another document developing any aspect of *Notes'* teaching, including the reference to Israel at VI, 25.

Evolution of Tradition a Slow Process

Eugene Fisher has identified the process by which these documents of the Holy See developed as one of *evolution.* He writes about an *"evolving attitude"* of the Holy See[36] and, in particular, an evolving attitude to the State of Israel.

Fisher sees the change in the Church's attitude to Jews and Judaism as a flowering of the biblical, liturgical, ecclesiological and even missiological movements that made Vatican II possible. He sees the changes as being an irreversible development of that dynamic inner life of the Church designated by the theological term *tradition.*[37] The slowness and cautiousness of each subsequent step, which can be observed in *Guide-*

lines (*1974*) and *Notes,* demonstrates, Fisher argues, the seriousness with which the topic of Jews and Judaism is approached by the Magisterium. Each step, he contends, even half-step, is measured and secured before the next step is attempted. Each step takes into account and builds upon previous statements. Fisher explains that while such a process might appear painfully slow to many in the dialogue, the result is increasing security and understanding. Furthermore he asserts that from the perspectives of pre-Vatican II history such progress as has occurred appears breathtakingly rapid.

Jorge Mejia's explanation of the process at work since *Nostra Aetate* concurs with Fisher's explanations. Changes, which are never sudden, Mejia explains, always have the authenticity of Apostolic Tradition to guarantee.[38] However, he maintains, when changes are made, in spite of slowness, the Church clings to them tenaciously because of what is acknowledged to be their Traditional authenticity. The Church is always concerned, he explains, to express deeper faithfulness to Apostolic Tradition, that is, to the Church's Apostolic origin, and the new outlook toward Judaism is *"more apostolic"* than the former.[39] The Catholic style, Mejia claims, is gradual, but when the Church comes to a decision it does not go back on it.

The evolutionary process in the Magisterial teaching which is observable over the past thirty years since the promulgation of *Nostra Aetate* is marked by this characteristic slowness.

The Dialogue with the Jewish People in the Total Perspective of the Renewal of the Post-Vatican II Church

There is another reason for the slow development in Catholic Magisterial teaching on Jews and Judaism which does not appear to have been taken into account by any commentators on the dialogue, and that is the vastness of the Catholic Church's endeavors to renew itself in contemporary times.

The wider perspective of the Church's life since the Second Vatican Council enables one to see that the teaching on Jews and Judaism which has evolved since the Council is but one area in a massive program of renewal through which the Catholic Church has been working. To indicate this fact is not to absolve or excuse the Catholic Church's tardiness in any given area of its undertakings or to disregard its innate conservatism and slowness. However, with a knowledge of the Church's modus operandi, it does help a little to understand the slowness of the process in making important statements.

POPE JOHN PAUL II AND THE STATE OF ISRAEL

A Review of Pope John Paul's Teaching on Jews and Judaism

It is to the disparate allocutions of Pope John Paul II that this study now turns in order to seek a fuller picture of the ordinary teaching of the Catholic Church on the subject of the State of Israel and its importance for contemporary Jews.

Throughout his allocutions to Jewish audiences and assemblies over the period 1979–1986[40] we find the Pope speaking about the special relationship, *the spiritual bond between the Church and the Jewish People* (12/3/79; 17/11/80; 28/10/85; *the living heritage, the common spiritual patrimony of Jews and Christians, as a present reality* (17/11/80; 6/3/8; 13/4/86). The Holy Father also emphasizes in his travels *the permanent validity of God's covenant with the Jewish people* (17/11/80; 6/3/82; 22/3/8; 26/11/86). He speaks about *the Jewish roots which remain deeply in the Catholic liturgy* (6/3/82; 6/7/84; 13/4/86), and *the need for these and other aspects of our common heritage to form part of the catechesis of the young* (6/7/84). The Pope also speaks, from personal experience, of having lived under Nazism in Poland, of *the malignancy of the ancient evil of Jew-hatred, Antisemitism* (12/3/79; 7/6/79; 31/5/80; 17/11/80; 25/4/83; 28/10/85; 26/11/86). He speaks about *the uniqueness of the Jewish experience of the Shoah* (12/3/79; 6/7/79; 31/5/80; 17/11/80; 5/10/80; 25/4/83; 28/10/85; 26/11/86). In his homily at Otranto he *linked the Holocaust and the rebirth of a Jewish State in the land of Israel* (5/10/82). Central to the Pope's vision of the Christian-Jewish relationship is the hope that it offers for *joint social action and witness to the One God and the reality of His kingdom as the defining point of human history* (17/11/80; 6/3/82; 22/3/84; 19/4/85; 13/4/86). He sees such joint action as the fulfillment of what is the mission of both Judaism and Christianity for promoting justice and peace which is the sign of the messianic age for both traditions. This way of collaboration in the service of humanity is a way of preparing for the reign of God, uniting Jews and Christians on a level that is deeper than the doctrinal distinctions which divide them.

From this survey it is obvious that Pope John Paul II's teaching on the subject of Israel is very slight, and, when compared to other subjects central to the dialogue on which he speaks, the teaching on Israel is most nuanced and at times ambiguous. The Pope concedes little on this issue, and it is not that he has not had opportunities to do so or that the subject was irrelevant at the time, because the issue has frequently been addressed to him in Jewish speeches.

At an audience for representatives of Jewish organizations on March 12, 1979, the president of the World Jewish Congress, Philip Klutznick, speaking about the *Guidelines (1974)*, stressed that

> in the long history of the Jewish people few events have been experienced with as much pain as the Exile, the separation of the people from the land promised by God. Never during this separation have the people of Israel lost their hope in the fulfillment of the divine promise.[41]

The Pope's reply acknowledges Klutznick's reference to *Guidelines (1974)* but makes no response to his pleading comment.[42]

At Manchester on May 31, 1982, the Chief Rabbi, Lord Immanuel Jakobovits, welcoming the Pope said that

> whilst enormous strides have been made defending Jewish-Catholic harmony, some items on our common agenda still remain to be resolved. They include the elimination of the last vestiges of religious prejudices against the Jews and some residual Christian hesitations in accepting the State of Israel as the fulfillment of millennial Jewish dreams.[43]

The Pope's reply reflects that he has heard Jakobovits' argument but on the specific issue of Israel it is very vague:

> I have followed your speech with great interest and I pondered the arguments you included in the speech. My answer is rather brief and not so full of arguments as your speech, but I am very grateful for your having put all these questions in your speech.[44]

In his capacity as president of the International Council of Christians and Jews, Dr. Victor Goldbloom addressed the Pope on behalf of the delegation on July 6, 1984. In his speech Goldbloom urged:

> Our concern for peace extends throughout the world; it has a particular locus in the Middle East. We must mourn every life that has been lost, Christian or Jewish or Muslim; and we pray that the State of

Israel and its neighbors may come to live in security, in recognition, and in fruitful rather than hostile relations. We invoke your leadership toward these ends.[45]

Pope John Paul II's response does not take up Goldbloom's special pleading for the State of Israel and its security and recognition but, rather, focuses on world peace:

World peace is built in this modest, apparently insignificant and limited, but in the end very efficient way. And we are all concerned for peace everywhere, among and within nations, particularly in the Middle East.[46]

In North America on February 15, 1985, the President of the American-Jewish Committee, Howard Friedman, elaborated in detail upon the State of Israel in his address to the Pope. He spoke about the non-recognition of Israel as an obstacle to peace in the Middle East and, quoting the Pope's remarks about Israel from *Redemptionis Anno*, urged him to take steps to formalize the diplomatic ties between the Holy See and the State of Israel and her people. He concluded:

Such a historic act . . . would be a watershed event in Catholic-Jewish relations. It would help create the sense of reality which is indispensable to peace. We would consider it a happy development of the decision of Vatican Council II. Above all it would be an act of profound spiritual and ethical significance in advancing the cause of world peace.[47]

In his reply, the Pope simply states:

I know also your concern for peace and security of the Holy Land. May the Lord give to that land, and to all peoples and nations in that part of the world, the blessings contained in the word "Shalom," so that, in the expression of the Psalmist, justice and peace may kiss.[48]

In the Jewish voices which address the Pope we hear the constant call for full political recognition of the State of Israel and of its religious and emotional significance for Jewish people the world over. But there is no significant response from the Pope, even though his attitude toward the State of Israel is generally positive.

Pope John Paul II's fullest expression toward Israel is to be found in

his Apostolic Letter *Redemptionis Anno* (April 20, 1984).[49] In no manner is this Letter a political speech or policy statement; it is a spiritual
challenge addressed to Catholics. It should be read within the context of
the many statements on Christian-Jewish relations and the Middle East
which have been issued by the Holy See and National Bishops' Conferences since the promulgation of *Nostra Aetate*.[50] In *Redemptionis Anno*
we find the Pope writing about the meaning of the Holy Land and the
Holy City Jerusalem for Jews, Muslims and Christians. Here he stresses
his great hope for reconciliation in that City. It is from this context that
he speaks about the State of Israel.

> For the Jewish people who live in the State of Israel and who preserve
> in that land such precious testimonies of their history and their faith,
> we must ask for the desired security and the due tranquility that is the
> prerogative of every nation and condition of life and of progress for
> every society.[51]

This statement constitutes an outright, clear, unambiguous affirmation
of the right of the Jewish State to existence and to security. It is a unique
statement among all of the Pope's statements. It exists in this Letter
without elaboration and is not elaborated upon in any other place.

Pope John Paul II on Israel: An Assessment

It could not be claimed that Pope John Paul II's attitude toward
Israel is negative nor that he is unaware or insensitive to Jewish sensibilities about the State of Israel. Questions remain, however, about the
once-only nature of his teaching about Israel and about the ambiguity of
his silences when the subject of Israel has been addressed to him. One
can understand the annoyance, frustration and even the suspicion which
is obviously experienced, as we have noted in Chapter II, by the Jewish
community in regard to the Pope's prudent silences.

THE POPE SPEAKS OF JUDAISM IN ITS RELATIONSHIP TO THE CHURCH

An assessment of Pope John Paul II's homilies, addresses and remarks by the criteria by which theological recognition for Israel is
sought, identified above, reveals that the Pope quite clearly continues in
the tradition of speaking about Judaism through a Christian perspective
which sees it primarily in its historical relationship to the Church and not
essentially as a religious entity in its own right. Though he speaks about

the permanent validity of God's Covenant with the Jewish people (17/11/80; 6/3/82; 22/3/84; 26/11/86) the Pope also describes Judaism as the root-stock of Christianity and of its liturgy (6/3/82; 6/7/84; 13/4/86), often situating it within the Christian heritage. Though these facts are the truth, they are also precisely representative of the comparative and subjugating view with its attendant biblical and theological notional explanations, to which, as we have seen in Chapter II, the Jewish partners in the dialogue object.

COMMON WITNESS, COMMON SOCIAL ACTION, COMMON HOPE

However, the Pope clearly does not relegate Judaism to a second-rate or superseded role. Rather, he sees the two religious systems as related, existing side-by-side, and called to a common witness and social action, and sharing a common messianic hope of the reign of God (17/11/80; 6/3/82; 22/3/84; 19/4/85; 13/4/86).

NO INDICATION OF THE RELIGIOUS SIGNIFICANCE OF ISRAEL

Nevertheless, in his references to the State of Israel, the Pope gives no indication that he sees in the return of Jews to the land of Israel and the rebirth of the Jewish nation any religious significance. He has come no closer to *"a theological recognition of the contemporary reality of Jewish national identity, and its centrality for contemporary Jewish being than the authors of Nostra Aetate, Guidelines (1974) and Notes."*

GUIDELINES ISSUED BY REGIONAL BISHOPS' CONFERENCES, AND BY PARTICULAR CHURCHES

The Nature and Purpose of the Episcopal Guidelines

Since the Second Vatican Council and *Nostra Aetate,* a number of guidelines redefining the relationship between Jews and Christians have been issued by the Bishops' Conferences of particular churches[52] throughout the world, and by official committees of particular churches, especially from the United States of America where there exists a high density of Jewish population. The purpose of these documents is pastoral. They arise from what appear to be immediate needs, issues and questions. They take their points of departure from *Nostra Aetate* and, also, in some instances, from *Guidelines (1974).* These documents are not theological treatises. Thus we find that in many cases major theological issues are simply not present nor raised.

The Common Characteristics of the Episcopal Guidelines

In all of these documents[53] we find condemnations of the antisemitism of the past and the present.[54] All urge a more intensive and wider dialogue.[55] They acknowledge the debt which Christians owe to Jews: the Scriptures; the liturgical heritage; key theological concepts such as covenant, messianism, and eschatology.[56] They speak of the necessity of explaining certain Gospel attitudes to the Jews and the Pharisees.[57] They look toward the hope of the common messianic age.[58] Most insist that the Jewish people as such were not guilty of the crucifixion and they ascribe Jesus' death to the sins of humanity as a whole.[59]

The general impression one has in considering these documents is that the Catholic Church in all parts of the world is searching for a new relationship with Jews and Judaism, one which is open, honest and full.

The Episcopal Guidelines and the State of Israel

Among the issues that appear least in these guidelines from regional and particular churches, or which are less fully developed where they do appear, are the Holocaust and the foundation of the State of Israel.

Some documents speak strongly about the centrality of the land of Israel to Judaism. The French Document (1973) acknowledges the land as God's permanent gift to the Jewish people.[60] The Austrian statement (1982) asserts that anti-Zionism is the latest form of antisemitism.[61] The Brazilian Bishops (1984—the only guidelines written with Jewish collaboration) speak about the rights of Jews to a calm political existence in *"the country of their origin."* Other guidelines acknowledge a deep sensitivity toward the land of Israel,[62] expressing a concern for Jewish rights to a homeland. Some documents include remarks about Arab rights.[63] The Los Angeles document (1977), and the Brooklyn guidelines (1979) speak about the great pride which American Jews have in the State of Israel and its achievements.[64]

While displaying open and positive attitudes toward the State of Israel and toward Jewish sensibilities to Israel, the documents also display an extremely prudential attitude. They say little more than we have already found in the documents of the Holy See and in the allocutions of Pope John Paul II.

The Episcopal Guidelines and the Theological Recognition Sought by Jews for Israel

THE PASTORAL PERSPECTIVES OF THE DOCUMENTS

Because the emphases of these documents is largely pastoral, concerning themselves with actual relationships between Catholics and Jews in the particular churches, and with issues (antisemitism; opportunities for dialogue; observing Jewish sensibilities) and problems (such as mixed marriages and common worship) which arise from such relationships, the documents treat of Jews and Judaism in a less notional fashion. The comparative and subjugating view of Judaism is still present (e.g. Diocese of Cleveland guidelines, 1979[65]), but it is less dominant because it is counter-balanced by pastoral concerns.

ENLIGHTENED VIEWS

The document of the Ecumenical Commission of the Archdiocese of Detroit (1979) contains a most enlightened direction vis-à-vis the terms on which Jews seek theological recognition for Israel, set out in Chapter III. They instruct that the dispersion of the Jewish people and their ingathering should be seen *"in the light of Jewish history and Jewish perspectives."*[66] The document goes on to speak about *"God's present favor to the Jewish people seen in their ingathering"* and suggests that Catholics interpret this through the biblical promises. This is a truly remarkable advancement toward that *theological recognition of the contemporary reality of Jewish national identity, and its centrality for contemporary Jewish being* which Jews seek. So also is the instruction given to Christians in the guidelines of the Diocese of Cleveland (1979). These guidelines teach that regard for Judaism should not be as for an ancient relic of the past.[67] This document acknowledges that God made the Jews his own and that he gave them an irrevocable vocation.

The U.S. Bishops' *Statement on Catholic-Jewish Relations* (1975) comes very close in its understanding of what Israel means for Jews when it speaks about *"an overwhelming majority of Jews . . . seeing . . . themselves bound in one way or another to the land of Israel."*[68] It also acknowledges that *"most Jews see this tie as essential to their Jewishness,"* instructing that Christians should *"strive to understand this link"* through studying Jewish writings and worship throughout two millennia which express the longing for their homeland.

EQUIVOCATION

Yet, paradoxically, the same document and its 1985 revision[69] give the impression of being not fully convinced of the religious importance which many Jews attribute to the creation of the State of Israel. Both documents contain an equivocating statement. In 1975: *"Whatever difficulties Christians may experience in sharing this view."* In 1985: *"Christians may experience difficulties in sharing views on such questions. . . . Appreciation of this link is not to give any particular religious interpretation of this bond."*

INCONSISTENT APPROACHES

In these documents we have observed an inconsistent approach to Jews and Judaism. Where we find that some authors, albeit a minority, advance toward a theological recognition of the contemporary reality of Jewish national existence and its centrality for contemporary Jewish being, others appear to be prudently cautious in their remarks about Israel and its place in contemporary Jewish life.

A SUMMARY OF THE MAGISTERIAL POSITION ON ISRAEL

In this chapter we have investigated alleged attitudes of the Catholic Magisterial teaching to Israel and to contemporary Jewish sensibilities about Israel by examining Magisterial teaching, and the following facts have emerged.

The Documentation of the Holy See

In regard to Israel and its religious interpretation we have observed how extremely cautious the framers of *Notes*, the only document which mentions it, have been. Recognizing how important Israel is to contemporary Jews, the authors have not committed themselves in the slightest to any possible religious interpretation. The document is highly prudent in this matter, and the evidence which we have considered above indicates that the Holy See appears to be waiting for further enlightenment and maturer understanding before it is prepared to say anything further about this matter. We have noted a major flaw in *Notes'* statement about Israel at VI, 25: the ambiguity of its added codicil. This is a feature of the document which demands explanation.

In the documentation stemming from *Nostra Aetate* there exists irrefutable evidence of the Catholic Church's high regard for the religion of Judaism and for Jews themselves.

Pope John Paul II

In the homilies, speeches and remarks of Pope John Paul II we have had an insight into his high estimation of Judaism and of its vital role, alongside Christianity, in the contemporary world. The Pope's empathy with the contemporary Jewish community is transparently obvious. He has a strong sense of the twin witness and action of Judaism and Christianity as both travel to and work toward the hoped-for reign of God.

On Israel and its religious meaning for Jews the Pope's prudence parallels that of the official documentation of the Holy See. We have observed that, addressed on this matter in the speeches of many Jewish leaders, the Pope has chosen to remain silent. We have also seen that his most empathetic statement on Israel in *Redemptionis Anno* is void of any religious interpretation of the State of Israel.

The Episcopal Guidelines

Since these documents derive from many parts of the world we would not expect to find a uniformity of understanding among them. We find instead a great variety of developing understandings which have their roots in *Nostra Aetate, Guidelines (1974)* and *Notes*. All the Episcopal guidelines hold contemporary Judaism in the highest esteem. All seek a greater knowledge and understanding of Judaism and deeper relationships with the Jewish people. All of the authors are concerned with these things as pastoral matters of great urgency. Some are concerned with particular pastoral problems as well. None of these documents has aimed at being fully developed theological statements; that is simply not their purpose.

On Israel and religious recognition there is barely advancement in the Episcopal guidelines, but there is much evidence of positive attitudes and openness, tempered by the characteristic official Catholic reserve, caution and prudence.

Jewish Terms for the Theological Recognition of Israel

In Chapter III we have noted the insistence of the Jewish theological challenge to the Catholic Church with its absolute lack of any specific direction other than the implication:

> It should not be a recognition of theological notions but a theological recognition of the contemporary reality of Jewish national identity, and of its centrality for contemporary Jewish being.

The evidence adduced in this chapter from the Magisterial teaching of the Catholic Church reveals that it has advanced moderately but cautiously toward the achievement of these terms of recognition, but that there is still a long way to go before they are fully achieved.

There is, however, a perceptible ambivalence in the Magisterial teaching. In some places the teaching expresses theological notional understandings, such as the religious attachment Jews have to the land of Israel expressed through biblical and liturgical sources.[70] Yet in other places it indicates the irrevocable vocation of the Jewish People (Cleveland, 1979) and that the "ingathering" is to be seen in the light of Jewish history and Jewish perspective. It mentions God's present favor seen in the ingathering (Detroit, 1979) and that most Jews see Israel as being essential to their Jewishness (U.S. Bishops' Statement, 1975).

An Assessment of Catholic Magisterial Attitudes to Israel and to Jewish Sensibilities about Israel

The evidence which we have considered above indicates that the most positive aspect of the Magisterial teaching about Jews and Judaism, in spite of its caution, reserve and prudence, is the growth since the Second Vatican Council of its openness in understanding and acceptance of Jews and Judaism, their religious experiences, and their contemporary religious role.

The epitome of this renewed Magisterial teaching on Jews and Judaism is focused in Pope John Paul II's allocutions. Here we find a strong sense of the continuing and contemporary role of the Jewish people, a strong sense of God's providential hand guiding them and Christian peoples to that ultimate convergence of history and destiny of humanity in the establishment of his reign. The Pope constantly emphasizes the permanent validity of God's covenant with the Jewish people with its widespread but as yet unspecified implications. While not explicitly acknowledging God's role in the events surrounding the creation of the State of Israel, the Pope certainly does not deny them when such suggestions are addressed to him by members of the Jewish community. He leaves the question wide open. He treats that matter with the same prudence which we have seen characterizing the documentation of the Holy See and the guidelines of particular and local churches. It is the same prudence which governs the Church's internal developments: the canonization of saints; the recognition of apparitions; the changes to her Canon Law, to her liturgy, and other matters of internal discipline.

Again we find the same openness, expressed with characteristic prudence, in the Episcopal guidelines. Some of these documents display significant advancement in their understandings of Jews and Judaism. The French guidelines (1973) affirm that Jewish election continues and thus also the Jewish vocation of the *sanctification of the Name*. They understand that Israel and the Church will co-exist until the end of time as a sign that the divine plan for humankind is not yet complete.[71] The German document sees Judaism and the Church working together for the realization of God's will in the world, thirsting together for justice and peace and for the final divine salvation, the resurrection of the dead and the life of the world to come.[72] The Brazilian document (1984) highlights the singularity of Judaism and its divine election and permanent vocation and witness in the world. It speaks of the convergence of Christianity and Judaism in the eschatological search.[73] This is highly enlightened teaching.

Refocusing the Problem

The achievements in the Catholic Magisterial understanding of Jews and Judaism since the Second Vatican Council and its difficult processing of the "Jewish Document" are by no means inconsiderable. Since that time there is evidence, adduced above, that the Catholic Magisterial understanding about Jews and Judaism is still developing. Its teaching, as evidenced above, is nuanced and prudent, but displays a profound openness. There are glimmers in some parts of that teaching of a developing understanding of what the return to the land and the rebirth of the nation-State of Israel means for contemporary Jews. Yet on this topic the Magisterial teaching is most cautious, displaying unwillingness to be confined to any particular interpretation of these events. Nevertheless there cannot be detected any hostility or negative animus toward Israel itself.

A reassessment of the nature of the problem of Israel in the dialogue between Jews and Catholics must take these advancements into account. More pertinently, such a reassessment must also take into account the Catholic Church's profound openness to contemporary Jews as having a tempering effect on the Jewish perception of the problem which sees the Church in its prudence and silences rejecting Israel and devaluing Jewish sensibilities.

Nevertheless, in spite of these positive factors, Magisterial silence on Israel, a deliberate and measured silence, constitutes a real threat to

Jews for Jewish existence itself. All that is left for Jews is to surmise that Catholics are less than sympathetic to their sensibilities concerning their existential security. This can be observed in two examples of ways in which Jews interpret such silence. First, *Rabbi R. Cohen* reports[74] that Pope John Paul II could not be faulted on Jewish-Christian relations during his 1979 U.S.A. visit, but that on Israel

> the Supreme Pontiff had put his enormous prestige and moral author-ity behind a set of shopworn, if not mischievous political ideas . . . 30 years behind the times, a policy of non-recognition that ill-behooved a Pope who strode so confidently across the international stage, and mischievous because the Pope's *refusal to even mention it by name* [*emphasis added*] could only encourage Palestinian resistance to the idea of Israel's rightful place in the Middle East—and perhaps even encourage terrorism against which the Pope spoke so eloquently.

Second, C. Krauthammer[75] comments on the way in which Pope John Paul II avoided any mention of Israel in his speech at the Synagogue of Rome:

> It is as if an Anglican leader came to a great meeting of reconciliation at the Vatican, spoke at length, and failed to acknowledge the exis-tence of the Pope. . . . The State did not merit a mention at the Rome Synagogue . . . it was right and good for the Pope to denounce anti-Semitism. But anti-Zionism—the threat to the safety and legitimacy of Israel—that is the Jewish problem today. . . . To address Jews purely as a religious community is to deny their peoplehood . . . this is what the Charter of the P.L.O. is committed to teach, that Jews belong to a religion, not a people (ARTICLE 20[76]). And religions have no claim to territory.

Such silence is an ecclesiastical prudence which begs to be explained fully to Jews, otherwise it will be continuously misconstrued by them. The Church's prudence and silence on the matter of the State of Israel as it is thrust to Magisterial attention by Jews time and again counteracts the immense advancements which have been achieved in the theological dialogue since the Second Vatican Council by confirming the Jewish opinion that there must be a serious theological reason for the silence, a reason about which Catholic authorities are being less than honest.

A reassessment of the problem of Israel must take the factor of the Magisterial prudent silence into account, seeing it as a serious flaw in

Catholic dialogical method. It must see this flaw's direct connection with Jewish existential insecurity.

The sole important measure for Jews is acceptance of the State of Israel. They do not perceive this as coming from the Catholic Church. Other developments in Catholic understanding and acceptance of Jews and Judaism are merely academic for Jews. All they effectively perceive is Catholic rejection of that which is of primary importance for Jews: their continued well-being and security which is inextricably linked with the safety and security of the State of Israel.

V. The State of Israel and Catholic Theology

In this and the next chapter we shall investigate whether theological recognition of Israel and the events surrounding its rebirth, which was cautioned against by *Notes* at VI, 25, is a problem for the Catholic Church, and, if not, then whether it is a possibility.

Here we shall explore whether theological recognition involves, as *Charlotte Klein,*[1] *Cornelius Rijk,*[2] and *Charles Angell*[3] and scholars from other Christian traditions suggest, areas of theology which are too sensitive for Christians in general and for Catholics in particular. It will investigate whether such recognition based in putatively sensitive areas of theology would be incompatible with Catholic theology and therefore the reason why the authors of *Notes* recommended:

> Christians are invited to understand this religious attachment which finds its roots in Biblical tradition, without however making their own any particular religious interpretation of this relationship (cf. Declaration of the U.S. Conference of Catholic Bishops, November 20, 1975). The existence of the State of Israel and its political options should be envisaged not in a perspective which is in itself religious, but in their reference to the common principles of international law.[4]

We shall investigate the writings of the above-mentioned scholars to discover how they perceive of the religious interpretation of Israel and the events surrounding its rebirth, and what they consider to be the sensitive and contentious areas of theology which retard Christian and in particular Catholic religious recognition of Israel.

There exists a small number of journal articles and other shorter works which indicate the need for Christian theological inquiry into the religious meaning of the return of the Jews to the land of Israel and the rebirth of the Jewish nation in the State of Israel.[5]

More comprehensive literary works treating of the theological issues surrounding the existence of Israel are rare, and they mainly deal with Israel in a tangential manner, being more absorbed in a quest for the contemporary hermeneutic of the biblical sources.[6]

We shall investigate these two categories of literature in the chronological order of their appearances.

The Shorter Articles

In a closely argued statement which aims at revising the place of the land of Israel within the framework of the Covenant in the life of the Jewish people, from a biblical perspective *John Oesterreicher* (1970) concludes that the significant event of the creation of the State of Israel, set against all odds and kept in existence against many threats and aggressive acts, is an act of God which all Christian theologians must come to acknowledge.[7] He argues that if the Christian theologian understands what has happened in Israel, then his attitude will transcend respect and admiration, and he will become a champion of the State's independence and integrity. Then the theologian will come to understand, as Oesterreicher has done, that Israel's success is not altogether due to the cunning of her statesmen and the superior strategy of her generals and soldiers, but rather to the "*outstretched arm*" (Exodus 6:6). Oesterreicher argues that Israel's future cannot be regarded by the theologian as a merely political problem and thus outside the competence of the theologian. He claims that the renewal of the people to the land might be seen by theologians as a wonder of love and fidelity, as a sign of God's concern for his people. Israel is the new proof, he claims, that God stands by His Covenant, that the last word lies not with the inventor of the "final solution" but with Him. Oesterreicher hastens to add that to say this about the State of Israel is not to sanction every decision of the Israeli government nor every action of the population. God's intervention nevertheless, he argues, could well go hand-in-hand with the mistakes of those to whom He shows favor.

Alan Davies (1972) directs Christian thinkers' attention to the State of Israel as a great act of Divine deliverance[8] after the ordeal of the Holocaust. Davies argues that the Jewish view of the State of Israel is endowed by the voice of Auschwitz with a certain messianic aura. It is a sign, he argues, that history still belongs to God because it signifies that Jewish survival, however tenuous, is still fact, visible and undeniable.

Davies comments on the skepticism of Christians regarding the claim by Jews that the Exodus-God, the Sinai-God, has again acted with the same hand of deliverance and the same voice of commandment in the arena of history, and this, in particular, with Israel's 1967 victory in view. Davies asserts that in this modern, new, revelatory event, Auschwitz is the commanding voice which precedes the redemptive act of the Jewish rebirth in Israel.

Davies notes the fact that Christians outside the fundamentalist frame of reference are hesitant to appeal to providence in contemporary history under almost any circumstance and are suspicious of others who interpret the complex events of the age in this transcendental light. He cites a particular instance of this recorded in *The Christian Century*—October 13, 1971, 1194—where such interpretations are put aside as non-acceptable. He thinks that the reason for this is that Christians have so terribly abused their own providential deductions concerning the vicissitudes of history in former ages not least with the Jews, whose diaspora was once regarded by the Church as divine punishment for their rejection. Davies thinks that they are not ready to risk further interpretations. Davies concludes that while a certain skepticism in the face of too facile a reading of current events against the tableau of eternal purposes is always healthy, at the same time an a priori denial that God and history are related in a real, subtle fashion is probably unhealthy and certainly unbiblical.

Charlotte Klein (1973) writes about the theological dimensions of the State of Israel. She is principally concerned with the silence of the Catholic Church.[9] Klein is convinced that there exists a basic theological reason for the Church's silence. She sees it aligned with the long-standing tradition which teaches that with the destruction of the Temple the "old" Jewish national independence must give way to the "new," the Church.

Klein has identified varieties of negative theology toward Judaism: (1) a strain of open hostility and bias toward Zionism; (2) a strain which has supported the re-establishment of the State of Israel as a preliminary step toward the final conversion of the Jews to Christianity; (3) a strain which espouses the anti-Judaism pronouncements of the Christian New Left.

There are, Klein argues, two important factors which must be recognized as being essential to Judaism. They are election and the promised land, both related to the Covenant. The land, she argues, has been crucial to the Jewish consciousness of identity. Furthermore, Klein insists that it is essential to consider Jewish self-interpretation in formulating an adequate theological perspective of Israel. A Christian theology of Judaism and of the State of Israel ought to take those dimensions into account, somehow balancing them with the doctrine of the universality of salvation through Christ.

Klein identifies two important "*theological dimensions*" which Christians should be mindful of in approaching Judaism. First, that Zionism and its achievements in the State was a providential "*salvation of Israel.*" That is to say that, because of Zionism, Jewry became conscious again of the inexorable fact of its separate identity, not merely as a religious body but as a people with a peculiar history and a special task in the course of history. Second, that Judaism is a living reality. It is, Klein asserts, a sign which Christians needed, a condemnation of their pseudo-theology of Judaism which goes back to at least the second century CE. Christianity, she explains, was not a substitute for Judaism nor the "new" Israel for the "old"; it is not a fossilized relic of Syrian society. The State is, on the contrary, proof of Judaism's dynamic vitality, of its right to exist and to choose its own form of existence, however ambiguous this may seem to pre-conceived Christian ideas. The State is evidence that Israel lives and that it is meant to survive, and that there is a power at work which ensures its survival as a separate ethnic and religious entity. It is this power within the people which assures their survival as Jews, in the face of all odds.

Klein concludes:

> Never again however must Christians impose upon the phenomenon of Israel their preconceived notions as to the meaning of its destiny. The Jewish people are capable of being their own interpreters.

Cornelius Rijk (1975) reports on a *Service International De Documentation Judeo-Chrétienne* (SIDIC) study session which had as its theme *People–Land–Religion in Jewish and Christian Tradition.*[10]

The symposium found that the theme *People–Land–Religion* is central in the dialogue between Christians and Jews but that it was the focus of much confusion and misunderstanding. It found that the return of the Jewish people to the land and the creation of the State of Israel, as not only a political fact but also as a religious event, was a strengthening of identity for many Jews but was a shock to many Christians who were thus faced with an entirely new and unexpected challenge.

After much scholarly debate, Rijk reports, the following conclusions were reached by the members of the symposium.

First, it was agreed that the link between people and land is basic to Jewish identity. Land is part of the Covenant between God and His people. The land is holy in itself but especially for the sake of the people. However, it was seen that in the Christian Scriptures the encounter with God is centered on the person of Jesus Christ, and therefore the land is of lesser importance. Thus, in those Scriptures, it was seen, the land and Jerusalem became a type of Christ. In the Patristic period typology lost contact with the underlying reality and therefore opposition was often created between the Jewish and the Christian concept of salvation.

Second, the symposium uncovered the fact that the Christian Scriptures do not give sufficient evidence of the early Christian attitude to the role of the land. The focus is on other models of biblical thought.

There emerged, third, the need to study the relationship between biblical tradition in the face of the contemporary question of the land.

Fourth, the scholars found that there exists a difference between Jewish and Christian concepts of peoplehood.

Fifth, the symposium pointed to the fact that the abstract nature of Christian theology does not contribute to a deeper understanding of the relationship between Christians and Jews seen in the perspective of salvation history.

A paper by *Clemens Thoma* (1975) emerged from the above-mentioned SIDIC Symposium. In it Thoma sets out to clarify, from a history of religions and a theological point of view, the unity and differences and discontinuity between the Hebrew Scripture and Christian Scripture statements on land, people and religion.[11] He does this, first, by an exposition of the afflictions and ideals of "*extra-testament*" early Judaism at the time of Jesus (170 BCE–140 CE) and, second, by taking into account interpretations of Christian Scripture statements on land, people and religion.

Thoma reaches the following conclusions. (1) The Christian Scriptures are deeply set in the milieu of the Judaism of Jesus' time. They refer to every religious style of life and convey the basic moods of the era. Sometimes, as was the case in contemporary Judaism, the Christian Scriptures stand in opposition to ideas and interests expressed in the

Hebrew Bible. (2) The Christian Scriptures make considerable corrections to the land–people–religion conception of life as presented in the Hebrew Scriptures. All reality is located around Christ and his *basileia*. They sublimate and symbolize, bringing things that were meant within history into connection with the absolute future. They ignore revisionist national tones. They distrust a piety based on the legalistic interpretation of Torah. (3) Thoma contends that efforts toward theological agreement with Judaism on the land–people–religion issue cannot be realized by biblical exegesis on its own. Additional theological systematic considerations are necessary. (4) Thoma indicates that a central question for all biblical and dogmatic considerations is Jesus a Jew who lived in the land of Israel and among the people of Israel. This is not to be taken as something merely external or coincidental. As a result of it there is, he asserts, a Christian duty of solidarity with the kinsmen of Jesus in the land of Israel today. He also notes that nowhere in the Christian Scriptures does Jesus pronounce against the national-religious attitudes of his day even though he is found to pronounce against the attitudes of the religio-militant Zealots. (5) Thoma argues that from the point of view of the Christian Scriptures one can understand that the Church is reserved toward messianic trains of thought in connection with the State of Israel. For those Scriptures the culminating point of the history of revelation was reached in Jesus. The Christian eschatology with its new order of cosmic dimensions no longer has its earthly center in Judaism alone but in the people of God consisting of Jews and Gentiles.

Kurt Hruby (1976), writing about the complexity of contemporary Judaism and indicating the problem of a multifaceted Judaism and Jewish identity in the contemporary world, sees the State of Israel, along with the recognition of the absolute oneness of God, as being the commonality of identity for all Jews today.[12]

Though, from the theological point of view, the State reproduces all the characteristic contradictions of Judaism, Hruby argues, and though Judaism itself is going through an important era of change, a period of investigation and seeking unity, the State of Israel is the center of unity for contemporary Jews. Hruby contends that it will become and is destined to be the spiritual center for the Jewish people.

Hruby argues that the quest for Jewish identity, focused on the State of Israel, must not be mistaken for nationalism, even if it momentarily looks like that, but that it is to be linked to Jewish existence.

Coos Schoneveld (1976) expresses the need for a Christian attempt to understand the religious roots and the spiritual basis of Jewish nationhood and to try to understand why for a Jew his spiritual commitment is so intimately connected with his being a member of the Jewish people, and why there is such an attachment to the land.[13]

Schoneveld argues that such an understanding is very difficult for Christians because Christianity claims to have transcended the level of national existence and territorial attachments and to have a more universal concept of humanity, in spite of the fact of history that the most extreme and excessive cases of nationalism and idolization of territory have occurred in the orbit of the *"Christian world."*

The author sees the source of Jewish nationhood in the Torah. He sees it as a nation of Covenant, the implications of which obliges it to conform to God's ways and to do what is right and just. The emphasis on nationhood in Jewish religion may, he argues, be interpreted as an attempt to relate God's will to the totality of the concrete existence of a nation with all its economic, social, political and territorial aspects. It is, he therefore argues, impossible to present Judaism and Zionism as two entirely different things. Zionism, he claims, is an important and valid contemporary expression of a fundamental dimension of Judaism. He writes:

> The basic aspiration of Zionism is freeing and uniting the Jewish people: freeing it from alienation, oppression and persecution, and uniting it in the Land from which it has been exiled but which it had never abandoned.

Alan Ecclestone (1980) writes about Israel's unique role among the nations of the world.

The problem of nationalism, he asserts, engages many peoples of the world as it is also engaging Israel. This struggle, Ecclestone argues, does not bespeak of Israel's vocation:

> Half a century of diplomacy, intrigue, warfare, economic pressure and tension only brings us to the threshold of questions which Israel raises both for the Middle East and the world.[14]

Ecclestone observes that at the heart of these questions is the fact that Israel's history insists that God does not let her go nor leave her; that His Covenant is, not was, the inescapable truth of the nation's experience. Thus, it is not as *"a nation"* but as *"the nation"* that Israel confronted the world. It is, he argues, her *"mystical character"* which grows more and more, not less impressive. It was, in Ecclestone's view, only when the nature of the Zionist enterprise was being defined by the great writers A.D. Gordon, M. Buber, and N. Goldman that Israel's mysterious character was brought into clear focus. He sees these authors as having urged that Zionism means much more than vigilance against attacks, and that Israel's present problems are not going to be solved unless their connection with her age-old calling is observed. These authors have taught, Ecclestone relates, that Israel's presence in the world is more important than her political stature, and that that presence should be marked by the purity of her witness to the divine intention.

Ecclestone inquires whether such a vocation stands up to the challenge of the twentieth century. He observes that Israel's struggles are not simply with her neighbors but with herself and in the depths of the nation's soul. Ecclestone warns that Christians must pray with Israel in this struggle, and if they do not, then they betray their own insensitivity to biblical history. He contends that what is being worked out in Israel today is a part of *"the titanic strife that embraces Jacob and Moses, Amos and Jeremiah, the passion of Christ and the Holocaust."* Christians fail wholly, he claims, if they fail to see the radical relation of the struggle to their being. Christians are involved, he argues, in that struggle: it is part of their own salvation history.

The real challenge for Israel and Christians, Ecclestone figures, is how to make Israel different from what it is today. To make it the champion of war, not against the Arabs, but against poverty, illiteracy and inequality; for the abolition of the sovereign state, and for peace. This, he claims (arguing along the lines of Goldman and Buber), is the essence of Zionism, and it is this that must be awakened in all, Israeli and Diaspora, Jewish hearts.

A messianic idea, claims Ecclestone, without a yearning for the redemption of the whole of mankind, without the yearning to take part in its realizations, is no longer identical with the messianic visions of the prophets of Israel. Neither can the prophetic mission be identified with a messianic ideal emptied of belief in the coming of the Kingdom of God. In pursuit of this, Ecclestone argues, Christians must go with Jews.

In an article in which he surveys the Holocaust and the State of Israel from a Catholic perspective, *Eugene Fisher* (1986) focuses upon a Catholic theological appreciation of the rebirth of a Jewish State in Israel. He suggests that Israel's Independence Day (Yom Ha-atsma-ut) should be a day for rejoicing for both Christians and Jews, a day of celebration and shared hope for the future.[15] Moreover, he continues, it should be a day of reflection for all, as believers, upon the meaning of historical events, especially the Holocaust and the State of Israel.

Fisher contends that Catholic appreciation of the significance of these events must begin by listening, in dialogue, to the ways in which the Jewish community has attempted to wrestle with them. He argues that the rebirth of Israel cannot be understood fully except against the background of the Holocaust. He believes that the meaning of Israel is a message of hope for peoples of all faiths. Its message is that tragedy, however seemingly implacable, need not lead people to abandon the struggle for survival in a post-modern world. That survival does not mean being petty and self-serving, but striving for the betterment of others. It also means that the cycle of victim and oppressor can be broken. Israel, Fisher contends, is an affirmation of life spoken amid the vivid memories of death. It is a cry of joy hurled in the face of doom, a statement of love that survived an abysmal hatred. The existence of Israel, he argues, is a symbol of hope and faith for all struggling people. Jew and Catholic, Fisher concludes, can share in affirming *"Ani Ma'amin—I believe, we believe in peace, in justice, in belief itself."*

In one part of his article *Bruce Williams* (1988) writes briefly, and therefore tantalizingly, about *"Redemption and the State of Israel."*[16] Williams raises the possibility of this issue for the Catholic theological agenda, arguing that an adequate Christian theology must see redemption in its tangible and transhistorical perspective, not just in a spiritualized and eschatological way. Because of the Church's teaching of contempt in regard to the Jews up until *Nostra Aetate,* it has not been possible for this matter to be on the theological agenda of the Catholic Church. Williams asks whether the Church could eventually come to acknowledge the rebirth of Israel as a sign of the times which carries positive theological meaning for Christians as well as Jews. Personally, Williams writes, his own Catholic faith commitment does not in the least inhibit him from embracing the political reality of Israel, with all its human limitations, as the pre-eminent embodiment of redemption here and now for the Jews, who always remain God's first love.

The More Comprehensive Works

James Parkes (1946–1954–1970) devoted most of his attention to an examination of the Jewish claims to the land. His work was to justify these claims on the basis of theological, historical and moral grounds.[17] Parkes believes that the Zionist experience was only one part of Israel's claim to statehood. The strongest case was to be made on other grounds. His efforts are directed toward showing that the Jewish land claims are based on a long religious and historical connection of some two thousand five hundred years' standing. It is, he argues, this connection, not in the twentieth century politics, that Israel can make the strongest claim to the land. Parkes is no biblical fundamentalist; he does not hold that God had made a direct gift of the land to the Jews but, rather, his focus is upon the role which the land has played in the development of Jewish theological identity. This is the crucial element, he contends, in any interpretation of the Jewish viewpoint. Parkes points out that it is primarily with this that non-Jews have such great difficulties with the Jewish point of view. And furthermore it is because non-Jews (Christians and Muslims) have no relationship to a land. Therefore, he argues, there is great necessity to explain the Jewish religious dimensions of the land to them.

Parkes sees that for Judaism the land is an essential part of the Covenant. It is the *Promised Land.* This is in contradistinction to the Christian notion of the *Holy Land.* For Jews it is the Holy Land because it is the Promised Land. For Jews there is an intensity of relationship with the land that does not exist for Christians or Muslims. This intensity, this "appeal to the land," has also involved for Jews the idea of return and resettlement. In this land, for them, there is an all-pervading sense of religious centrality that just does not exist in other lands. This, Parkes claims, is the key for understanding the Jewish point of view. The full implications of the land for Jews, he argues, are reflected in the very nature of the Jewish religion which is a community oriented religion. It has as its heart a natural community whose whole emphasis is focused on man as a social being relating to others through righteousness and justice. The other fact is that Judaism has little concern with the afterlife: its concern is with life in the world, life in community. In the Scriptures, Parkes indicates, the Covenant included the promise of a land in which Israel could be a nation and a people, and from biblical times forward, he asserts, that land has been Palestine. Thus, he argues, the history of the people cannot be divorced from this geographical and historical setting. The soil of Palestine is unique for Jewish thought and life, even for secular Jews. This link, Parkes claims, is not something of the past but is of the future: all the promises concern the future.

Parkes contends that Judaism is concerned with roots, with physical existence and geographical activity, quite unlike other religions. The entire history of the Hebrew Bible, he maintains, ties it to a single people and the actuality of a single land. The ebb and flow of all the biblical narratives are steeped in this reality. Its laws and customs are based in the land and its climate. Its agricultural feasts and festivals follow its seasons. Its historic festivals are linked to events in its history.

Parkes argues that the uniqueness of Jews' relationship to the land is an essential part of Jewish life and identity that Jewish historians take for granted, and that is precisely why they did not write about it. It was a neglected issue that became a problematic issue when Arab nationalism began to challenge the Zionists. It was only after this, Parkes contends, that the matter became of paramount importance.

The Jewish case, he argues, rests on a history little known even to many Jews. Parkes therefore presents Israel's claims by stressing the unique historical relationship which the Jews have had with the land. In this way he hopes to quash the idea that the Jews took land that was not theirs, as well as demonstrating this long historical connection in the core of the Jewish claims. Thus Parkes writes about "*the five roots of Israel.*" The first three roots are concerned to establish the land in Jewish tradition: (1) Judaism as the religion of a community; (2) the messianic hope, intimately connected since the destruction of the Jewish State in 70 CE with the expectations of a return to the Promised Land; (3) Jewish history and the long experience of dispersion and insecurity. The remaining roots are concerned to establish the physical links with the land, and they are (4) the continuity of Jewish life in Palestine since 70 CE and (5) the unique relationship between the Jewry of Palestine and the whole Jewish people. From these five roots Parkes constructs his position concerning Israel's right to exist as a nation among nations in the Middle East.

In his argument Parkes dismisses the charge that Israel is a creation of Western Imperialism and that Jews took land from the Arabs. He points to the fact that there has been a continuous Jewish presence in the land for centuries. This root is not religious and, therefore, it cannot be dismissed by atheists or secular critics. He argues that Jews had always struggled to preserve their presence in Palestine and that over centuries there had been an immigration flow. He claims that the Zionists were a new type of immigrant, but not unique.

Parkes argues that secular Zionists express a feeling inherent in Judaism and that, in spite of their rejection of religious orthodoxy, they are really the heirs of deep-seated feeling for the whole people implanted by religious orthodoxy. He argues that Zionism is unintelligible without a complete understanding of how the land is intimately linked with Jewish identity and survival. He argues that Zionism is not just a Western version of Jewish nationalism. That Zionism became politically active in the nineteenth century is, he claims, more an accident of timing than of necessity. Zionism, he contends, manifests impulses long in existence in Judaism: the historical situation of Jews contributed to its manifestation at a particular time. Parkes believes that Zionism has been its own worst enemy by not giving enough attention to root 4, the continuity of Jewish life in Palestine since 70 CE. He writes:

> But one thing has been constant, a determination to maintain roots in the "Promised Land." Much of the modern discussions of Zionism would have been clearer if this had been realized. It was no case of "Jews returning to a land they had left two thousand years ago." As a people they had never left it either physically or spiritually. The remnant actually dwelling in it might be very small, but it was always thought of as an earnest people as a whole, and it was always entitled to be supported by the people as a whole. All through the centuries Jews had tended to return to it, now individually . . . now in groups of tens or hundreds.[18]

Walter Harrelson analyzes the land theme in the Hebrew Scriptures in four stages: the promise and the gift of the land,[19] life upon the land, the threat of the land's loss, and the land in God's promises.

In this fourth stage, the land in God's promises, Harrelson focuses upon promises in the Hebrew Scriptures which center upon the restoration of the fortunes of Israel, all of which include or imply a return to the land of Canaan and in particular to Zion. The author proceeds to treat briefly the various hopes that find expression in the prophetic eschatological texts because, he claims, they are at the very heart of Israel's understanding of the land.

Harrelson explains that prophetic eschatology does not mean a mere restoration of things as they were. All of the passages containing pictures of God's consummation have new elements of how things shall be. The images that stand out are of a new royal figure; a new Zion; a new Exodus and re-entrance to the land; a new heart and spirit; a new Covenant; a new heaven and earth; a new Day of Tabernacles and a new concord among the world powers. Harrelson is struck by the earthiness of the images and their focus upon the actual needs of human life upon the earth. Later, he observes, Christian and Muslim tradition will make this material into something otherworldly, centered beyond physical existence and beyond this earth. However, in its life-situation this prophetic eschatology is earth-centered and concerned with human needs and long-ings. It makes the point, he argues, in a variety of ways that God does not let the divine promise fail of realization. Even with the failings of the elect people, and though the divine promise of consummation and new-ness of life on earth is long in coming, God will not finally be undone, and his sovereign will shall be performed.

Harrelson asks whether the establishment of the State of Israel can be entirely separated from these promises. It is his belief that it cannot be so separated. The author argues that, first, it needs to be borne in mind that such promises held in faith have their immediate and enduring power and effect in the community that holds them. He contends that eschatol-ogy is always to some extent realized eschatology. Second, he argues that the existence of the State of Israel has to be traced to these texts as a partial source of the visions of the Zionists who in the nineteenth and twentieth centuries labored and suffered for the establishment of a home-land for the Jewish people. Also, he informs his reader, these visions were behind the readiness of non-Jews to see and respond positively to the import of the Zionist's struggles. Harrelson warns that though the State of Israel is not to be identified with the messianic community promised by biblical prophecy, it also is not just a secular state.

Harrelson concludes by warning that if Christians do not take into account the mysterious and religious dimensions of the land of Zion, if they do not keep in mind what Zion and the land mean to secular as well as religious Jews, then they will not only be unfaithful to the actualities in Israel, but they will also dishonor this heritage to be found in the Hebrew Scriptures. The Land, he contends, is God's gift to an Israel loved by God. It requires fidelity in Israel's care of it, in the way life is lived upon the Land. Though its loss may be threatened, God keeps bringing Israel back to this place, for here is to be the scene of a new and glorious transfiguration of life and death, with the holy land and Zion as the center of the transfiguration.

A SYNTHESIS OF THEOLOGICAL IDEAS
RELATING TO ISRAEL

In the literature we have surveyed above there exists a profusion of theological questions, suggestions and ideas which are related to the land of Israel, to the return of the Jewish people to that land, and to the rebirth of the Jewish nation and its significance for contemporary Jews.

There is no single, dominant interpretation of these events, though the writers' ideas often converge. There is nothing here which could be regarded as a Christian theology of Israel.

The events are seen as a *divine deliverance,* a *redemption of Israel* by Oesterreicher, Davies, Klein, and Williams. Klein and Williams argue that the reborn Israel is *proof both of a divine favor and of a divine plan for Israel.* Oesterreicher, Ecclestone, Williams, Parkes and Harrelson view the rebirth as a *sign of God's fidelity to His Covenant with Israel.* Davies and Ecclestone speak about the *messianic aura* and the *messianic nature* of modern Israel. Davies, Oesterreicher, Klein, Williams and Harrelson see in the events of the return and rebirth of the Jewish nation a *strong sign of God's continuing role and supremacy over history.* Davies regards these *events as revelatory.* Klein reads them as a *sign of the Jews' special role in history, a role designated by a divine plan.* Hruby warns that the *events surrounding the restoration of the nation are not to be taken merely as a form of nationalism.* Schoneveld is more explicit in speaking about *the religious roots and spiritual basis of Jewish nationalism.* Ecclestone cautions *against interpreting Israel as a merely political presence* in the world. Ecclestone and Harrelson regard the return and rebirth as *an eschatological event.* Ecclestone goes further, with Fisher, to contend that *the event has repercussions for the whole of humankind.* Fisher regards it, linked with the Holocaust, as a *sign of hope for humanity, and especially for all victims of oppression.* The sign indicates *God's victory over the powers of evil.*

SENSITIVE THEOLOGICAL ISSUES?

As a result of our investigations in this chapter, the following theological issues emerge as being possible factors of theological sensitivity underlying Christian and, in particular, Catholic reluctance to give theological recognition to Israel and the events surrounding its rebirth:

- Is contemporary Christianity skeptical about the role of Divine Providence in contemporary history? (Davies)

- Can contemporary Christian theology accommodate an inclusive view of redemption which would see the possibility of incorporating contemporary Jewish events focusing on Israel into the Christian event of salvation *through Jesus Christ?* (Harrelson, Ecclestone, Fisher, Klein, Williams)

- Could the events surrounding the creation of the State of Israel be acknowledged as revelatory by Christians? (Davies, Klein, Hruby, Schoneveld, Ecclestone, Fisher)

- Is it possible that Christian theology might come to see the return of the Jews to their ancient homeland and the rebirth of Jewish nationhood as events of realized eschatology? (Davies, Ecclestone, Harrelson)

- Can Christian theology accommodate Zionism?

In the next phase of our investigation we shall inquire whether these theological propositions are incompatible with Catholic Magisterial teaching and therefore the source of the perceived theological problem in the dialogue.

VI. Major Hurdles for a Catholic Theology of the State of Israel

Here we shall seek to refocus the problem of Israel in the Catholic-Jewish theological dialogue by testing the veracity of the assertion that the cause of Catholic Magisterial prudence and silence on the topic of Israel is that theological recognition involves issues, of the nature indicated in the theological propositions represented by the questions at the conclusion of Chapter V, which are incompatible with Catholic Magisterial teaching.

TESTING THE SENSITIVE AREAS FOR CATHOLIC THEOLOGY

Is Contemporary Christianity skeptical about the role of divine providence in contemporary history?

Alan Davies' observation is not vacuous. Among the contemporary churches of the Reformation tradition (and Davies belongs to this Christian tradition) he may well observe a *"reluctance to appeal to providence in contemporary history under almost any circumstances."* During the twentieth century there has been an ever widening secularization within many of these churches, and this has affected their theologies. Secular-humanist thought strongly exists in many of the Reformed Churches of Western Christianity. Such thought is epitomized in the British Broadcasting Corporation's production *Sea of Faith* which was written, presented and narrated by the Reverend Dr. Don Cupitt, Dean of Emanuel College, Cambridge.[1] Cupitt's secular-humanist thought has no place for the existence of divine providence.

In his presentation Cupitt argues that a profound mutation has been taking place as religion breaks free from the outworn supernatural beliefs that at present stifle it. He presents the view that religion itself is simply human, concluding:

> God (and this is a definition) is the sum of our values, representing to us their ideal unity, their claims upon us and their creative power. Mythologically, he has been portrayed as an objective being, because ancient thought tended to personify values in the belief that important words must stand for things.[2]

Cupitt claims that the meaning of "God" is religious, not metaphysical. The true God is not God as a picturesque supernatural fact but God as our religious ideal. He argues:

> When we have fully accepted these ideas and have freed ourselves from nostalgia for a cosmic Father Christmas, then our faith can at last become fully human, existential, voluntary, pure, and free from superstition. To reach this goal is Christianity's destiny, now approaching.[3]

If it is Christian skepticism of a similar nature to Cupitt's which Davies observes and of which he speaks, then he is partly correct in his assessment that "*Christians outside the fundamentalist frame of reference are hesitant to appeal to providence in contemporary history under almost any circumstances.*" Such a Christian perspective would be unlikely to view the return of the Jews to their homeland and the rebirth of the Jewish nation as "*a great act of deliverance*" or as "*a sign that history belongs to God*" or that "*the Exodus-God, the Sinai-God, has again acted.*" Skepticism about the existence of a personal God, let alone His continuing role in history, would prevent such an interpretation of the events surrounding the creation of the State of Israel. Such a Christian perspective would hardly be inclined to respond to contemporary Jewish events in a theological manner at all, but more likely in a political one.

The Implications for Catholic Theology

However, Davies' statement is a generalization. There are many Christian traditions which cannot be said to fall into this category,[4] and the Catholic Church is one of these. This is abundantly apparent from the survey of official Catholic teaching in Chapter IV where it has been established that the official teaching contains a profound sense of God's continuing activity in the history of the Jews.

In Pope John Paul II's allocutions there is a strong sense of God's providential hand guiding both the Jewish and the Christian peoples to that ultimate convergence of history and destiny of humanity in the establishment of God's reign (17/11/80; 6/3/82; 22/3/84; 19/4/85; 13/4/86). While not explicitly acknowledging the divine initiative in the events surrounding the creation of the State of Israel, the Pope certainly does not deny them when such suggestions are addressed to him by members of the Jewish community, but he leaves the question wide open. We have observed that he appears to treat the matter with the same prudence which we have seen characterizing the documentation of the Holy See and the guidelines of particular and local churches. It is the same prudence which governs the Church's internal developments: the canonization of saints; the recognition of apparitions; the changes in her Canon Law, to her liturgy, and other matters of internal discipline.

Can contemporary Christian theology accommodate an inclusive view of redemption which would see the possibility of incorporating Jewish events focusing on Israel within the Christian event of salvation *through Jesus Christ?*

This suggestion involves a revisionary approach to Israel's role in the plan of redemption. It would refocus the Christian covenant within the entire framework of covenant theology to see it more sharply as a further expression of the Abrahamic–Sinaitic covenant tradition. This would be a return to the primitive Christian theology of covenant expressed in the Pauline literature at Galatians 3:15–18, where Paul stresses that the covenant with Abraham is fundamental to subsequent covenants. The implication of such a covenant theology is that a further covenant does not annul a former one but confirms and enhances it (cf. Ephesians 2:12). The Pauline view is inclusive of the Abrahamic–Sinaitic covenants of which he has a highly positive view (cf. Romans 9:4), seeing the "old" (Sinaitic) covenant inhering in the "new" (Christic) covenant.

It was post-Pauline Christianity, wounded by the decisions of the Sanhedrin at Javneh,[5] in which the theology of annulment and replacement in relation to Jews and Judaism developed, of which the Letter to the Hebrews is the epitome.[6] It is there that we find in an ad hominem argument the clear annulment and replacement view of the "*first covenant and its ordinances*" (Hebrews 9:1–10) which became the basis of "old" and "new" annulment and rejection theology and the typological developments of the Patristic era. Williams, who proposes this idea, has said unequivocally that his personal view is that the political reality of

Israel (in spite of its human frailties) is the pre-embodiment of redemption here and now for the Jews who remain God's first love. Harrelson views it as an event of realized eschatology. He and Ecclestone write about the *"mystical"* character of Israel, a *"presence"* which is more important than political status. Ecclestone speaks of a *"witness"* which the presence of Israel bears for the twentieth century. It is a witness bound up with *"titanic events"* (the Holocaust) which parallel the passion of Christ. Fisher contends that Israel, through the interlocking events of the Holocaust and the rebirth of the nation, is a *"symbol of hope"* for all who are oppressed and downtrodden. Doubtlessly, all of these expressions indicate the writers' sense of awe in the face of the contemporary Jewish events, but only Klein and Williams identify the events as *"redemptive,"* that is to say, as the work of divine initiative, as part of the divine plan of which the Christian event is regarded as the culmination.

The Implications for Catholic Theology

The Patristically originated and long-enduring theology conveyed by the expression *"extra ecclesiam nulla salus"*[7] has been eclipsed by official Catholic theology in favor of a return to a more universal outlook, such as that expressed by Paul in the Letter to the Romans (8:19–23). There Paul emphasizes that the experience which Christians now possess is but the first-fruits (foretaste) of that full redemption whose scope will embrace all history and nature. This theology was reformulated by the Fathers of the Second Vatican Council in the *Pastoral Constitution on the Church in the Modern World* (#45) where it is written:

> While helping the world and receiving many benefits from it, the Church has a single intention: that God's kingdom may come, and that the salvation of the whole human race may come to pass. For every benefit which the People of God during its earthly pilgrimage can offer to the human family stems from the fact that the Church is "the universal sacrament of salvation" simultaneously manifesting and exercising the mystery of God's love for man.

> For God's Word, by whom all things were made, was Himself made flesh so that as perfect man He might save all men and sum up all things in Himself. The Lord is the goal of human history, the focal point of the longings of history and of civilization, the center of the human race, the joy of every heart, and the answer to all its yearnings. He it is whom the Father raised from the dead, lifted on high, and

stationed at His right hand, making him the judge of the living and the dead. Enlivened and united in His Spirit, we journey toward the consummation of human history, one which fully accords to the counsel of God's love: "To re-establish all things in Christ, both those in the heavens and those on the earth" (Ephesians 1:10).[8]

This statement is the basis for a contemporary inclusive theology of redemption which would see contemporary Jewish events incorporated within the Christian event of redemption through Jesus Christ (*"the goal of human history, the focal point of the longings of history and civilization . . . the answer to all its yearnings . . . the consummation of human history,"* the *"re-establishment of all things in Christ"*). This idea of inclusive redemption in no manner contradicts or detracts from Catholic soteriology, the doctrine of redemption through Jesus Christ. It is inherent in that theology at its most fundamental and primitive level, in the Sacred Scriptures. Such an inclusive view of redemption would in no way subjugate the redemptive nature of contemporary Jewish events but, on the contrary, it would view them with wonder and with awe because of their divine origin and impetus. From a Jewish viewpoint such doctrine would also appear to accommodate the view expressed in the Seder Liturgy that *"redemption is not yet complete."*[9]

Could the events surrounding the creation of the State of Israel be acknowledged as revelatory by Christians?
Davies has specifically acknowledged these events as being revelatory, while Klein, Hruby, Schoneveld, Ecclestone and Fisher have all strongly hinted that they read these events as signs of divine revelation.

The Implications for Catholic Theology

If the events surrounding the rebirth of the Jewish nation were to be regarded by the Catholic Magisterium as *redemptive,* in the manner in which this has been discussed above, then the answer to the question must be in the affirmative since Christian and Jewish scripture and theology always acknowledge redemption as being a divine initiative. Both traditions also acknowledge through their scriptures that redemptive activities are the supreme moments of divine revelation.[10]

The Christian belief that in Jesus Christ God's full and definitive self-revelation is available to humanity in no way precludes the possibility of continuing divine revelation. Nor does such a belief find difficulty with the possibility of continuing individual "moments" of divine revelation, be they Christian or otherwise. Such "moments," after the due process of discernment, in the case of the Catholic Church, by the Magisterium, may well be incorporated into what Christians acknowledge as the full and definitive "moment" of God's self-revelation in the person and work of Jesus the Messiah. By this way of reckoning, all revelatory "moments" have an inner unity. That is to say, they all interlock into that one great Christic "moment." This teaching flows from the Fathers of the Second Vatican Council who reflect on the "moments" of divine revelation as they have been experienced by the Hebrew and Christian traditions, in the following way:

> Through this revelation, therefore, the invisible God . . . out of the abundance of his love speaks to men as friends . . . and lives among them . . . so that He might invite and take them into fellowship with Himself. This plan of revelation is realized by deeds and words having an inner unity; the deeds wrought by God in the history of salvation manifest and confirm the teaching and realities signified by the words, while the words proclaim the deeds and clarify the mystery contained in them. By this revelation then, the deepest truth about God and the salvation of man is made clear to us in Christ, who is the Mediator and at the same time the fullness of all revelation.[11]

Though the redemptive "moment" in Christ is definitive and complete, the *"history of salvation"* of which the Council Fathers speak is continuing and the *"deeds wrought by God,"* whether of the past, the present, or those of the future, still have that *"inner unity"* as they continue to be revelatory throughout the generations succeeding the Christian "moment."

In the theology of revelation, Jewish and Christian, God Himself is always the initiator and object of revelation. In these contemporary Jewish events, the various Christian writers above have suggested that again God has revealed Himself as divine deliverer (Oesterreicher, Davies, Klein and Williams), as Lord of history (Klein, Davies and Williams), as the One faithful in His love for His people, Israel, His first love, faithful to His covenant with them (Oesterreicher, Ecclestone, Williams, Parkes, Harrelson and Davies). There appears to be no theological reason why the Catholic Magisterium should not give the same recognition to the events surrounding the rebirth of the Jewish nation.

Is it possible that Christian theology might come to see the return of the Jews to their ancient homeland and the rebirth of Jewish nationhood as events of realized eschatology?
We have already heard Bruce Williams speak about Christianity's transcendental view of redemption which traditionally held that the redemption of Israel must wait until the end of human history. Clemens Thoma has also written about Christianity's eschatology with its new order of cosmic dimensions and which no longer has its earthly center in Judaism but in the people of God consisting of Jews and Gentiles. Coos Schoneveld has identified a Christian problem with particularism in relation to contemporary events which Jews identify as redemptive. The problem lies in the fact that traditional Christian doctrine focuses on universal not particular redemption.

The Implications for Catholic Theology

There is little doubt that such modes of theological thought would have constituted insurmountable obstacles for Christians generally and for the Catholic Magisterium of former generations if they had been faced with this idea. However, in the light of a revised inclusive theology of redemption such as we have seen above, which gathers all human history and events, all human longings and yearnings, into the Christic "moment" of redemption, it is very unlikely that it would be possible to view the return of the Jews to their ancient homeland and the rebirth of the Jewish nation in the State of Israel as anything less than a *sign of the times* and thus as an event of realized eschatology of a messianic nature. Acceptance of contemporary Jewish events on this basis would be totally consistent with a theological perspective which marked the formative era of the Christian Scriptures.

The general view emerging from the Christian Scriptures is that the messianic age has come within the present world order. This thought receives striking expression in Paul's phrase that "*the ends of the ages are coming*" (1 Corinthians 10:11). Paul's teaching about the ages is that there are two: the present, and that which is to come. Christians live in both ages, which is another way of saying that the new messianic age has been inaugurated in Jesus, though it still awaits its consummation at the end of the present age (Matthew 13:39, 40, 49; 28:20; 1 Peter 1:9). Now to comprehend the Christian teaching, it must be understood that these two ages do not stand in an order of temporal succession. The peculiarity of the human situation is that, though people live in *chronos* (measurable time), *kairos* (the unmeasurable time of God's reign) is upon them. This is the burden of Jesus' teaching about the new reign (*basileia*) of God which had appeared with his coming, as it is recorded in the Gospels.[12]

The interplay between *chronos* and *kairos* is filled with *signs/signs of the times* (evidences of the presence of *kairos*) to which Christians are exhorted to be alert. Such *signs/signs of the times* are messianic "moments" of revelation pregnant with God's presence and activity.[13] This is the basis of Catholic eschatology, and the suggestion in question is in no way at odds with that.

Can Christian theology accommodate Zionism?

This question is raised explicitly and implicitly by a number of the Christian writers whose works we have reviewed in this chapter and in other places in this study. C. Schoneveld argues that Zionism and Judaism are inseparable, that Zionism is an important and valid contemporary expression of a fundamental dimension of Judaism. Secular Zionism is, Schoneveld contends, a necessary stage in the process, and it must ultimately give way to the religious heritage wherein is the true identity of Jewishness. R. Brashear has insisted that Christianity must be openly Zionist in its expressions and that this implies a commitment to a nation-state for the Jewish people in the land of Israel. J. Oesterreicher claims that if the Christian theologian understands what has happened in Israel, then his attitude will transcend respect and admiration and he will become a champion of the State's independence and integrity.

The Implications for Catholic Theology

Zionism appears as a broad spectrum ranging in nature from a secular political movement to a deeply religious belief.[14] In its essence it is essentially "*that profound longing for the fullness of Jewishness which can only be attained by the return of the Jewish people to the land of the promise.*"[15] The reality is that the "*profound longing*" embraces the entire spectrum of Zionism, secular, political, religious. The question arising is whether Catholic theology can accommodate this reality.

If Schoneveld's view that Zionism and Judaism are inseparable is true, the fact then is that if Catholic theology cannot accommodate Zionism, then neither can it accommodate Judaism because Zionism, as will be seen in Chapter VII, is an inseparable characteristic of Judaism. It is precisely this fact that many of the Jewish commentators in the dialogue, whose works were surveyed in Chapter II, were contending. This fact is at the heart of the Jewish threefold challenge to the Catholic Church which was identified in Chapter III. It is this fact which is fundamental to the reasoning which seeks theological recognition for Israel in terms of *"the reality of how Jews are today"* in the light of the Jewish return to the land of Israel and the rebirth of the Jewish nation in the State of Israel. In other words, what is being sought is a theological recognition for Israel as an existential reality fundamental to Jewishness.

It would appear to be this reality with which the Catholic Magisterium has most difficulty. At least, it is not clear in the official teaching, evidenced above, that the Magisterium understands Zionism in terms of its existential urgency for Jews in the contemporary world. It clearly recognizes the right of Jews to a homeland in Israel but it also clearly divorces the State of Israel from that recognition, treating it as being in some manner extraneous to Jewish existence, a merely political entity, the product of a political movement, viz. "Zionism."

If the Magisterial attitude were to be corrected in its understanding of the absolutely central and existential role which the State of Israel plays in the life of universal Jewry, then it would come to an understanding of the essential role of Zionism for Jews.

THE EVIDENCE WEIGHED

The evidence which we have considered here indicates that these theological propositions, apart from the one focusing on Zionism, pose no difficulty for Catholic theology in that they are alien or contradictory to Catholic doctrine. Furthermore, it also indicates that such theological propositions should not be regarded as constituting reasons which might prevent the Catholic Church from accepting the Jewish theological challenge which was identified in Chapter III.

More positively, the evidence in this chapter indicates a vitally important role for Jews and Judaism in Catholic theology not by way of patronizing concession but because Jews and Judaism have an integral and indispensable role in the continuing divine plan for the redemption of the human race.

The evidence produced here also indicates that one must seek some other-than-theological explanation for *Notes'* statement that

> Christians are invited to understand this religious attachment which
> finds its roots in Biblical tradition, without however making their own

any particular religious interpretation of this relationship (cf. Declaration of the U.S. Conference of Catholic Bishops, November 20, 1975).

The existence of the State of Israel and its political options should be envisaged not in a perspective which is in itself religious, but in their reference to the common principles of international law.[16]

VII. The Internal Jewish Dialogue on the State of Israel

Pursuing further clarification of the problem posed by Israel in the Catholic-Jewish dialogue we shall now seek to elucidate sources of Jewish understanding about Israel. In so doing we shall discover that new evidence will emerge which will give us a radically different slant on the problem of Israel in the Catholic-Jewish dialogue.

Listening to the Internal Dialogue on Israel

A number of Christian writers,[1] the *Guidelines (1974)*,[2] and the Guidelines of the National Conference of Catholic Bishops[3] direct attention to Jewish sources as being possible loci for discovering Jewish self-understanding and, by implication, places to discover Jewish understanding about Israel.

Zionist Literary Sources

The Christian writers—and the official Catholic documentation—who suggest the consultation of Jewish sources do not provide directions to any particular Jewish literary source of self-understanding apart from the liturgy. Presumably they mean to indicate Jewish literary sources which focus on land–people–religion themes, and these are to be found in the literature of Zionism.

The focus of the following investigation will be Zionist literary sources and Jewish liturgical texts. Its purpose will be to determine their usefulness as a means of "listening" to the internal Jewish dialogue on Israel, and of seeking how Jews themselves understand the events surrounding the foundation of the State of Israel.

THERE IS A FUNDAMENTAL DIFFICULTY IN CONSULTING JEWISH LITERARY SOURCES

Those who would inquire of Jewish sources in order to understand how Jews interpret the State of Israel become immediately aware of a serious problem when listening to Judaism's inner dialogue. This problem is Judaism's inner diversity represented in the broadest terms by both the secular and the religious spheres. In the latter it is marked by fundamentalism and non-fundamentalism and divided into ultra-Orthodoxy, Orthodoxy, Conservatism, Reconstructionism, and Reform.

One finds that in the entire Jewish panorama there is no Jewish central authority to consult. There is no one authoritative body secular or religious. Consequently it is not possible to find sources for investigation which could be said to be authoritative or normative, or even representative of Jewish interpretation of Israel. This is a fundamental difficulty for those who would consult Jewish literary sources.

THE RETURN TO ZION: THE COMMON VISION

Zionism in its modern sense was born in August 1887 when the First Zionist Congress adopted Theodor Herzl's *Basle Programme* which declared that "*Zionism seeks to secure for the Jewish people a publicly recognized, legally secured home in Palestine.*"⁴ Nevertheless, Herzl and the Congress did not start from scratch. They were preceded not only by 1,900 years of yearning for Zion on the part of Jews who were scattered among the nations, but also by earlier nineteenth century writers who broached the idea of the return of the Jews to their ancient homeland, and even by some modest beginnings of practical colonization in Palestine.

The Hebrew expression *galut* (diaspora) conveys the Jewish concept of the condition and feeling of a nation uprooted from its homeland and subject to alien rule. It is unique to the history of the Jewish people that this feeling has powerfully colored the emotions of the individual as well as the corporate consciousness. The sense of exile was expressed by the feelings of alienation in the countries of the diaspora, the yearning for the national and political past, and persistent questioning of the causes, meaning and purpose of the exile.

In the liturgy the yearning for the Land of Israel and particularly for Jerusalem finds powerful expression. It is toward Jerusalem that the Jew turns when he prays, and three times daily he beseeches God: "*Gather us from the four corners of the earth; to Jerusalem, Thy city, return in mercy . . . rebuild it soon in our days. . . . May our eyes behold Thy return in mercy to Zion.*"⁵ The two most solemn occasions of the year, the Passover Seder and the Day of Atonement, reach their climax in the proclamation, *"Next year in Jerusalem."*⁶

The two fathers of modern Zionism, Moses Hess and Theodor Herzl, reflect this age-old longing for the end of *galut.*

MOSES HESS

The political vision of the national regeneration of the Jewish people which Hess set forth in his book *Rome and Jerusalem* (1862) was his motivating force.⁷ Hess envisaged the day when Jews must participate in the great regeneration of nations which started with the French Revolution. Nevertheless, his view of the community which they would build in Egypt and Palestine was very firmly inspired by Torah principles.⁸ Hess tells his readers that for him the symbol of Jewish nationalism was the sight of his grandfather weeping for the ruined Temple at Jerusalem on the Fast of the Ninth of Av, and praying with utter conviction for its restoration.

THEODOR HERZL

If we look carefully at Theodor Herzl we shall see that as a child of the Enlightenment his Jewish religious background is predictably lacking. Yet even so, the concept of *Messiah* and *Galut* was known to him and made a strong impact in a childhood dream which he later remembered and recounted:

> One night, as I was going to sleep, I suddenly remembered the story of the Exodus from Egypt. The story of the historical Exodus and the legend of the future redemption which will be brought about by King Messiah became confused in my mind. . . . One night I had a wonderful dream: King Messiah came. . . . On one of the clouds we met the figure of Moses . . . and the Messiah . . . turned to me: "Go and announce to the Jews that I will soon come and perform great miracles for my people and for the whole world."⁹

However, though the Messianic-Galut idea was in his subconscious, Herzl reached his solution to the Jewish problem of his day through a political and sociological approach: the establishment of a *Judenstaat,* a secular vision.

In a similar manner to Hess and Herzl, other Jews, sharing in the common hope for the in-gathering of the exiles and the establishment of the community of Israel, suggested parallel solutions through secular ideologies.

THE JEWISH DIALOGUE ON ZIONISM:
THE ORIGINS OF DIVERSITY

The ferment of Zionist ideologies expressed in these one hundred years prior to the foundation of the State of Israel in 1948 was influenced by the living conditions and philosophies of the two distinctly separate Jewish communities, one in Western and the other in Eastern Europe. In the course of time and in the cause of Zionism the ideological differences between these communities merged and ultimately fused together. Nevertheless, both sources deposited their seminal characteristics which became part of the total tapestry of ideological Zionism and which continue to be discernible in Judaism's contemporary internal dialogue about the nature and function of the State of Israel.

The Eastern European Zionist Tradition

In the Eastern European Zionist tradition, which was largely unaffected by the secularization of the Enlightenment and continued to be nourished by a vital Rabbinical-Jewish tradition, Zionist statements have a pronounced religious character.[10] A good example of this is to be seen in *The Manifesto of the Bilu*.[11] This is a document written in Constantinople in 1822. The *Biluim* were about five hundred young people, mainly from the Kharkov region in Russia, who were part of a wider movement of the *Hovevei Zion* ("Lovers of Zion"). The *Manifesto* is fundamentally a religious statement having Isaiah 2:5 as its inspiration. Its vision is to end the great exile, and to re-establish the *House of Jacob* in its *own country* (Palestine). It climaxes with the statement, *"Hear, O Israel! The Lord our God, the Lord is one, and our own land Zion is our one hope."*

The Western European Zionist Tradition

On the other hand, the Zionist tradition of Western European Jewry presents a very different character, being predominantly secular and political. Products of the Enlightenment, Jews in Western Europe had discarded many aspects of their Jewish culture and religious tradition for the sake of assimilation.[12] Typical of this tradition is Theodor Herzl's *The Jewish State* (1896).[13] Quite unlike *The Manifesto of the Bilu*,

Herzl's statement is motivated by the political situation of Jews in Western Europe and by the insidious evil of antisemitism which manifested itself in ever new forms of oppression and persecution. It is a plan to create a sovereign State for Jews on a purely political basis which would allow Jews total autonomy and safety.

Differing but Complementary Views

These statements from two separate "movements" of European Jewry, though expressed differently, aim ultimately at the same ideas: (1) the end of diaspora existence, and (2) the re-establishment of the "House of Israel." The Bilu version, religiously motivated, has the land of Palestine clearly in view as being the milieu for these ideas, while the Herzl view, politically motivated, speaks only of a "state" with no particular geographical locale identified: that would come later. The views are in no way mutually exclusive, nor are they incompatible. They are both dependent on that Jewish dream which focuses on the in-gathering of the Jewish people and the re-establishment of the community of Israel.

The Triumph of Secular Messianism

The Zionist dialogue with its dichotomy between religious and secular ideologies, as it moved toward the creation of the State of Israel, retained at its center the dominant vision of the in-gathering of the Jewish people and the re-establishment of the community of Israel. Though the State of Israel was ultimately the product of secular–political ideologies, definitive canonical status was given to the traditional religious ideas of the religious Zionist vision in the *Proclamation of Independence.*[14] There we find such references as: *"the spiritual homeland of the Jewish People"*; *"from whence they gave the Bible to the world"*; *"the Exile"*; *"the principles of liberty, justice and peace as conceived by the Prophets of Israel."* The Proclamation contains the appeal *"to stand by us in the great struggle for the fulfillment of the dream of generations for the redemption of Israel."* It finally concludes, *"With trust in the Rock of Israel, we set our hand to this Declaration."*

The Opponents of Modern Zionism

Although the great majority of Jews in the modern era have supported Zionism in one way or another, some have rejected it outright, while others have demonstrated serious reservation concerning the idea in its political forms.

ORTHODOXY AND ZIONISM

Groups of Orthodox Jews throughout the modern Zionist period had rejected Zionist theology, and many had resisted any attempt to force the "redemption" of Israel through human means. They regarded such action as the usurpation of divine prerogative.

A major manifestation of this reaction to modern Zionism was articulated by a Polish group of Orthodox created by some leading rabbis. They were known as *Agudat Yisrael*.[15] This organization manifested a profound distrust of the Zionist idea and discouraged its members from returning to Palestine to take part in the Zionist enterprise there. These Jews were prepared to wait for the Messiah, and they were unwilling to act unless a clear sign was given them from heaven. They were also highly suspicious that Zionism was merely the offspring of the Emancipation which represented to them an alien life-style incompatible with the demands of Torah. As they watched the Zionist idea developing, they saw that it would require individual Jews to surrender their Jewish identity to the collectivity of a nation which, like any other secular nation of the world, was to determine its life-style by the norms of twentieth century civilization.

REFORM AND ZIONISM

In 1812 *David Friedlander,* a banker and one of Prussia's richest and most influential Jews, and a disciple of *Moses Mendelsson* the founder of Jewish reform, reflecting the mood of many Jews of his day, called for a radical denationalization of Judaism. Friedlander published a work entitled *About the Rebuilding Mode Necessary by the New Organization of Jewry in Prussian States with Reference to Worship, Religion and General Education—A Word for This Time.* In this work Friedlander argued that the time had come for Jews to remove from their worship all yearnings for Palestine, Jerusalem, and the restoration of the ancient Temple:

> Here I stand before God, I pray for blessing and success for my King, for my fellow citizens, for myself, for my family—and not for a return to Jerusalem, not for a restoration of the Temple.[16]

Friedlander's basic motivation for this change was Jewish assimilation. He aimed to eliminate those elements in Jewish life and worship which made the Jew different from any other European. He wrote:

As long as the Jews were, if not actually persecuted, at least regarded as strangers and treated as such . . . as long as they were not only made to feel—but were actually told—that they were only tolerated and that they really belonged to Palestine, so long was there neither cause nor reason to change the contents and the language of prayers.[17]

This attitude was reflected as early as 1819 in the prayerbook of the Hamburg Reform Society which deleted or altered the traditional prayers calling for the in-gathering of the exiles in Eretz Israel. Some later Reform prayerbooks went further and eliminated from the ritual even such seemingly innocuous phrases as *"the remembrance of Jerusalem, the Holy City."* The Pittsburgh Platform of 1885 expressed the reform position succinctly:

We consider ourselves no longer a nation, but a religious community, and therefore expect neither a return to Palestine . . . nor the restoration of any laws concerning the Jewish State.[18]

Reform's position hardened at the time of the First Zionist Congress. Then the American Association of Reform Rabbis declared their total disapproval of any attempt to establish a Jewish State.

The Reform position remained thus until the rise of Hitler. Since then Reform's stance on Zionism has undergone radical change. At its Columbus Convention in 1937 the Central Conference of American Rabbis (Reform) affirmed the obligation of all Jewry to assist in the upbuilding of Palestine as a Jewish homeland.

RELIGIOUS REACTIONS TO POLITICAL ZIONISM

Not all religious Jews were unwelcoming of modern Zionism but some gave strong opposition to nakedly secular-political Zionist ideology believing in the in-gathering of the exiles and the establishment of the community of Israel in terms of a spiritual nation solidly built upon Torah.

Representative of such opposition is the scholar and rabbi, *Solomon Schechter*. In Schechter's theological vision of the Kingdom of Heaven, the in-gathered (redeemed) and nationalized Israel plays a central role.[19] The Kingdom of Heaven and the Kingdom of Israel converge: Israel being itself the microcosm of the Kingdom of Heaven in which all the conditions of the Kingdom of Heaven are to find concrete

expression. However, Schechter insists that the Kingdom of Heaven/
Israel is not political:

> The patriarchs in the minds of the Rabbis did not figure prominently
> as worldly princes, but as teachers of the Kingdom. The idea of theoc-
> racy as opposed to any other form of government was quite foreign to
> the Rabbis.[20]

Schechter's Zionist vision is of a Jewish nation gathered in Jerusalem
established on the Torah and its teaching. It is a vision devoid of any
secular political notions.

Franz Rosenzweig, philosopher and theologian, argues against political Zionists who thought of Judaism as only a form of nationalism:

> In order to keep unharmed the vision of the ultimate community, (*the
> Jewish People*) must deny itself the satisfaction the peoples of the
> world constantly enjoy in the functioning of their state. For the state is
> the ever-changing guise under which time moves step by step towards
> eternity. So far as God's people are concerned eternity has already
> come . . . for the nations of the world there is only the current era.[21]

The philosopher and theologian *Martin Buber's* messianic reading
of Zionism, though he was not an Orthodox Jew, is a counterweight to
political and cultural viewpoints. He envisaged the Return to Zion as a
means to bring to life again the primeval Jewish relationship to God, the
world, and to humankind.[22] For Buber, the Return to Zion in the twentieth century signifies a renewed attempt to fulfill the mission for which
Israel was elected. Buber claims that the encounter with the land is
primarily an existential encounter between Israel (and ultimately all
people) and God. He argues that it is not simply a matter of replanting
the national organism in its natural soil and allowing it to grow. The
relationship with the land is a covenant relationship, and it is consequently burdened with risk, tension and responsibility. The bond between Israel and Zion is thus seen by Buber as a mystery.

THE UNITY AND DIVERSITY IN THE PRE-1948 DIALOGUE

The dichotomy between religious and secular Zionist ideologies,
though sharing as their common vision the in-gathering of the exiles and
the establishment of the community of Israel, are the two divergent

poles of the pre-1948 dialogue on the Zionist idea. These encompass a full range of Zionist ideological expression such as follows.

THE PHILOSOPHICAL-THEOLOGICAL TREND.[23] This grouping includes those writings which are systematically philosophical-theological in nature rather than being publicist or ideological. These writers deal with such issues as Jewish peoplehood as a purely religious community and as an ethic, national entity with its own cultural and spiritual dimensions. Representative of this trend are *Yehudah Alkalai*,[24] *Zvi Kalischer*,[25] and *Franz Rosenzweig*.[26]

THE ZIONIST-IDEOLOGICAL TREND, which divides into two subdivisions:

(1.) *the writings of political Zionism* focus on the need for a homeland for the Jewish people as the only solution for their problems. While most see this homeland in Israel, others do not require this to be the case, arguing that any land in which Jewish statehood can be achieved would suffice. These are represented by *Theodor Herzl*,[27] *Max Nordau*[28] and *Leo Pinsker*.[29]

(2.) *the writings of cultural, spiritual Zionism* which are focused in Jewish peoplehood rather than in territorial and political solutions. These emphasize Judaism as a system of values and patterns of living, seeing diaspora existence as an inescapable fact of Jewish reality. They argue that survival depends on finding a solution for the Jews' ongoing diaspora existence. These opinions are represented in the writings of *Ahad HaAm*.[30]

The distinction between these two divisions is that the question for political Zionism is the problem of the Jews, while for cultural Zionism it is the problem of Judaism.

THE CULTURALIST AUTONOMIST TREND, which is the other side of the coin of the cultural, spiritual Zionist trend. The fundamental difference between them is that the former affirms exclusive diaspora existence while the latter sees a need for a settlement in the land of Israel. This trend secularizes Judaism so that it becomes a system of concrete cultural patterns and values. It does not require a specific homeland and the full sovereignty of the state for the Jewish nation, but instead affirms diaspora existence, encouraging the Jew to completely assimilate into the host-nation. Its main thrust is to protect the cultural distinctiveness of Jewish peoplehood. This trend is represented in the writings of *Simon Dubnow*.[31]

THE SOCIALIST TREND, which is literature concerned with the socialist question, where the Jewish question enters the picture within this underlying context. This trend divides itself between the socialist formulations that are Zionist (represented by the work of *Moses Hess*[32]) and those which are virulently anti-Zionist and diaspora affirming as represented by *the Bundist movement*.[33] Both see the Jewish people as charged by its vocation (made clear by the prophets of Israel who call for justice and right living, sharing of wealth, and compassion for the poor and destitute) to fulfill the Socialist ideal. This requires sovereignty, the machinery of state, and also a geographical location so that the ethnic group can express itself in the economic-political dimension. However, with some notable exceptions, it does not require any particular geographical location for this purpose.

THE MYSTICAL TREND. These writings contain mystical formulations of Judaism, and they distinguish themselves from the more secular views of other trends. They affirm both the category of Jewish peoplehood and the category of land, and specifically the land of Israel. They can be divided thus: (a) formulations which adhere to Orthodox religious expression (represented by the writings of *Abraham Isaac Kook*[34]) and (b) those formulations which vis-à-vis Orthodoxy can be characterized as non-religious as represented by the works of *Aaron David Gordon*[35] and *Martin Buber*.[36]

ACTIVE IDEOLOGICAL TREND. That is, those ideologists who were the immediate architects of the State of Israel as represented in the writings of *Meir Bar-Ilan*,[37] *Vladimir Jabotinsky*,[38] *Chaim Weizmann*,[39] *Abba Hillel Silver*,[40] and *David Ben-Gurion*.[41]

This survey of modern Zionist literature indicates that behind the rebirth of the Jewish nation in 1948 lay a century of spiritual and intellectual ferment focusing on Jewish identity, existence and survival in the modern world, all of which produced Zionist philosophy with its pluriform expressions in nationalist, socialist, religious and revolutionary ideologies.

The survey also demonstrates the fact that in attempting to "listen" to this early internal dialogue on people–land–religion in its state of nascent flux, one must contend with a wide range of idiosyncratic Jewish thinking.

THE INTERNAL JEWISH DIALOGUE AFTER THE HOLOCAUST AND THE CREATION OF THE STATE OF ISRAEL

The dialogue of the contemporary era takes place with the Jewish Holocaust and the creation of the State of Israel as its background, two realities which give it an entirely different character to the earlier dialogue.

The Holocaust and the Creation of the State: Surprise Events in Jewish History

Both events appear to have seized contemporary Jewish existence by surprise. The Holocaust occurred at a time when the fruits of Jewish Emancipation had appeared to have ripened, when the Jews of Europe had seemed to have achieved assimilation and acceptance to an historically unprecedented degree. They were then to learn in unimaginable ways that seemingly liberal and fair-minded Gentiles were prepared to lend their support, sometimes actively and sometimes passively, to the many atrocious antisemitic manifestations that gradually led to the "Final Solution." Suddenly the horror of apocalypse was a reality in contemporary Jewish history. This shattered all the ideals and aspirations that Emancipation had symbolized.

The establishment of the State of Israel, long hoped, worked and suffered for, was of premature birth, brought on by a fortuitous combination of events in the decisive vote of the United Nations General Assembly on the Partition of Palestine on November 29, 1947 and the sudden end of the British Mandate in Palestine on May 14, 1948.

Holocaust and Israel—Dual Foci of the Dialogue on Jewishness and Jewish History

The surprise nature of these events in the drama of Jewish existence has had a shock effect on Jews and has understandably given rise to subsequent decades of introspective Jewish dialogue about the meaning and purpose of Jewishness in the contemporary world and of recent Jewish history, with both the Holocaust and the State of Israel as central issues of the agenda.

The Shock of the 1967 and 1973 Israeli Wars

As a result of the Six Day War in 1967 and the Yom Kippur War in 1973, when again there was a further shock to Jewish existence in the contemporary world, there has been an escalation in the dialogue on Jewishness and Jewish history.

Rabbi Abraham Heschel contends that in 1967 the brutal threat of deadly danger to the existence of the people and the State brought about a deep reawakening of the Jewish soul:

> We were carried away by an awakening of the soul, overwhelmed by a vision of the profound seriousness of Jewish history. Suddenly we sensed the link between the Jews of this generation and the people of the time of the prophets. . . . We are that very same living people, part of the body of Israel of all generations.[42]

The discovery for Jews was that

> Jewish history has not come to an end. Many of God's blessings are still in store for all mankind. The State of Israel is a prelude, we hope, to new wonders, to new blessings.[43]

Harold Fisch, head of the Institute for Judaism and Contemporary Thought, also detects that as a result of the events of the Wars of 1967 and 1973 there is a revolutionary movement among Jews involving a renewal of the bond with the land of Israel and a revived sense of the Jewish people's unique role in the world.[44]

The Diversity and Complexity of Opinions about Israel in the Contemporary Dialogue

THE DIALOGUE IN ISRAEL

The late *Uriel Tal* provides in his report a glimpse of the diverse and complex nature of the internal Jewish dialogue in Israel.[45]

Tal indicates that countless discussions about Israel take place among its population but especially among young Israeli intellectuals who attempt to contemplate the theological and eschatological and existential meaning of the historical concrete reality which is the State of Israel. Tal outlines two approaches which approximate to the poles in the pre-1948 dialogue between which exist further ideologies. First he describes the *Political Messianic Trend* which is based on a fundamentalist hermeneutical approach to passages of Scripture, particularly *Exodus 13:17–17:6* which furnishes a political ideology to settle the land of Israel by conquest. From this point of departure, the essence of which is in the normative, absolutist authority and the sanctified significance bestowed upon the conquest, not simply the settlement of the land, there emerges a conception of the State of Israel as a redemptive phenomenon. According to this point of view the State of Israel and its wars are evidence of a process of redemption which is taking place today by natural and supernatural means. This gives a mystical authority to the State. A second form is the *Existential Trend* which is to be detected in the self-searching among groups of youth of senior high school and university ages. It is particularly noticeable in kibbutz-born Israelis of the second and third generation who were brought up with little sense of their Jewishness, of their culture, history or religion, and who are now awakening to their heritage and coming to a new self-awareness. These young people are preoccupied with the meaning of Jewish existence. Tal indicates that the more sensitive among them are questioning the justification for a Jewish sovereignty in Palestine. He sees in this group an inner conflict regarding their identity as human beings, as Israelis and Jews. In their view, Tal relates, granting statehood the status of eschatology would necessarily bring about the horrors of political messianism that the modern world has known since the French Revolution. The non-Orthodox in this group think that the State should be regarded not as an ecclesiastical institution but solely as a social, juridical entity. They see its purpose being involved in the realization of human rights and duties such as the affirmation of one's physical, personal, intellectual freedom; in the preservation of one's individuality despite the leveling and conforming impact of modern civilization and the actual practice of one's sovereignty as an individual citizen.

A DIVERSITY REFLECTED IN SCHOLARLY WRITINGS

In the writings of contemporary Jewish scholars from Israel and the diaspora there is further evidence of the contentious nature of the internal Jewish dialogue. Here we find widely divergent and even mutually exclusive ideas. For example, the following writers interpret the existence of Israel as a religious phenomenon and are concerned about its fundamentally secular state.

Nathan Rotenstreich (1966) writes about what he conceives as one of the most urgent issues facing the State of Israel: What part should religion play in the life of the society and State? What is the nature of the relationship between the institution of the State and that of organized religion? The author sees these as salient, practical issues. He does not attempt to answer his questions but rather to further the issues at stake.[46]

Yehudi Adam (*1980*) makes a ravaging attack upon Zionism, modernism, the concept of Judaism as religion, and contemporary forms of Jewish identification and loyalty. All are described as distortions of the "true Judaism" of the past. The author suggests that no recovery of this time of "true Judaism" is possible. His definition of Judaism is of a spirit springing from a vision of the world that is free from man-made evils.[47]

Paul Eidelberg (*1987*) discusses the "right-wing" view of Israel as a theocratic enclave. He concludes that Israel's governing elites have abandoned the Torah and authentic Zionism for a specious pluralism. He contends that only halakhah can truly legitimize the State of Israel and justify the Jewish people's possession of their ancient homeland. He also asserts that the time has come for Israel to draft a true Declaration of Independence rooted in Torah.[48]

In stark contradiction of these expressions of religious concerns, other scholars are concerned to maintain the secular character of the State against religion.

Samuel Schafler (*1981*) argues that modern Zionism represents an event as radical discontinuity in Jewish history owing little to Jewish religion and strongly opposed by authoritative religious spokesmen and leaders. Modern Zionism, therefore, he argues, represents a radical break with religious Jewish tradition, and this accounts for its secular and political character.[49]

Michael Langer (*1987*) presents the case for secularism in Israel. He argues that the separation of religion from the State is necessary if Israel is to realize its Zionist destiny as a crucible for the development of new ways in Judaism, ways compatible with modern thought as understood by the humanist tradition of the Western world. Langer argues that Israel cannot afford to have Rabbinic Judaism neutralizing the Jewish State as an instrument for Judaism to confront modernity. The sooner religion and State are separated, in his view, the better for the renewal of cultural Zionism. The sooner Israel renews a pluralistic cultural Zionism, according to this author, the greater the prospect that the unique venture in human history, which began some 4,000 years ago with the call of Abraham to go forth into the land, will generate a call that can be heard by the contemporary generation as well.[50]

The Intense Concern for Jewish Existence and Identity Expressed in Contemporary Jewish Literature

In these writings we can see how closely Israel and the issues which surround it are associated with concerns for Jewish identity in contemporary history. *Adam* inquires whether it is possible to recover Judaism's "true identity" since the triumph of secular Zionist ideologies. *Schafler* is concerned to show how Zionism has radically changed Jewish identity.

Jewish existential and identity issues are commonly expressed as concerns by contemporary writers, as will be apparent in the following reports.

W. Fein (1973), writing about *the Zionist dream versus the reality of the State of Israel,* deals with what he considers is a crucial problem, the relationship between the dream of Zion and the reality of the State of Israel. From his analysis the author draws upon important conclusions for the relationship of world Jewry to the State of Israel.[51]

Norman Levine (1974) writes about *the changed nature of Jewish existence, especially in the Diaspora, since the establishment of the State.* He maintains that the establishment of the State of Israel has radically transformed the character of Jewish life outside its borders. He argues that "diaspora" cannot be properly applied to Jewish communities after 1948 and that at the very least the term would require drastic reinterpretation in view of the fundamental change in the political realities. He analyzes the position of various mechayyevai hagolah, *"Yea sayers of the Diaspora,"* notably Dubnow, Ahad Ha-Am, and Buber, from this critical perspective.[52]

Chaim Waxman (1976) reports *how reluctant-Zionist Jews in America conceive of their identity* in exposing what he contends is a crucial problem: the relationship between the dream of Zion and the reality of the State of Israel. From his analysis the author draws upon important conclusions for the relationship of world Jewry to the State of Israel.[53]

Ben Halpen (1980) describes *the essence of Jewish identity.* He denies that there is any specific body of ideological content or any code of practice, however broadly and literally construed, that constitutes "the essence of Judaism." What makes Jews Jewish, he claims, is their possessing a symbol-set that is uniquely Jewish, being derived from their own civilization. Not the content of Judaism, he contends, but its symbols unite modern Jews with each other and their past. One remains a Jew as long as one does not abandon these symbols, be they concepts, acts or objects. These symbol-sets of Judaism, he argues, are religious in origin and character.[54]

Sidney Schwartz (1986) expresses *the need to redefine the concept of Zionism in order to revitalize Jewish life.* He gives his analysis of the present status of Zionist ideology, asking: When did Zionism lose its meaning? He traces, briefly, its history from dream to politics and suggests a redefinition of the concept to make it serve the vitalization of Jewish life and the enhancement of its moral quality both in Israel and the diaspora.[55]

Gordon Tucker (1988) expresses *the need for a basic philosophy of Zionism and Judaism,* arguing that the plethora of problems confronting Israel in its internal affairs, political, economic and religious, in its foreign policy and its relationship to diaspora Jewry, cannot be understood, let alone solved, without a basic philosophy of Zionism and Judaism. To this end Tucker presents the works of two writers, Benjamin Ravid and James Diamond who give, in Tucker's view, *"brilliant and consistent views of Israel's role in the modern world,"* even though their positions are diametrically opposed.[56]

Vital Existential Issues Underpin Ideological Issues

Emerging from this survey of literature from the contemporary dialogue is the fact that in the internal Jewish dialogue on Israel existential issues frequently underpin ideological ones. These issues concern the meaning of Jewishness in the contemporary world, the interpretation of the catastrophic and momentous events of twentieth century Jewish history, and the security and acceptance of Jewish people in their pluriform existence in the contemporary world and into the future. All of these concerns converge on Israel which is the unifying symbol of hope for Jewish peoplehood in the contemporary world.

RELIGIOUS JEWS AND THE STATE OF ISRAEL

Among religious Jews there are widely differing approaches to the State of Israel, of which the following are representative.

NON-RECOGNITION AND REJECTION

Some ultra-Orthodox do not recognize the State of Israel as having any religious significance.[57] Among them are Israelis, particularly some of the residents of *Mea Shearim,*[58] notably the *Neture Karta* (literally, "guardians of the city"). They would recognize only a divinely inaugurated state with its constitution rooted in Torah.

THE STATE-MYSTICAL AUTHORITY

Some Orthodox, presented by Uriel Tal as the *Political Messianic Trend,* view the State of Israel as having a redemptive mission and a mystical authority. These are the *Gush Emunim* (literally, "Fidelity Bloc"), a religious activist movement which centers on graduates of the Benei Akiva Yeshivot, and which has attempted to establish settlements in Judea and Samaria in defense of the right to settle the whole land of Israel. One of its basic points of departure is that Israel's wars are to be considered *milhamot mitzvah,* wars which constitute religious obligation. This group argues that the commandment of the Torah at Exodus 23:29–30 concerning the Seven nations are applicable to the Arabs today in Eretz Yisrael.

THE STATE: MYSTICISM AND MESSIANISM

Yet other Orthodox and some Conservative Jews view the State of Israel as having a mystical messianic property. This point of view is elaborated by the Jewish authors Rabbi Abraham Heschel and Professor Harold Fisch.

Heschel sees the State as an answer to the age-long prayers of Israel which are so strongly resonant in its liturgy.[59] Heschel demonstrates how Jews who share this belief use the Jewish liturgy as a hermeneutical tool for their understandings of Israel. He refers to the two-thousand-year-long mourning for Zion and Jerusalem which is focused in the liturgical life of Judaism, both public and private. He sees the State not as the fulfillment of the longings expressed in these prayers but as making the messianic promise, hoped for in these prayers, plausible. According to Heschel the presence of Israel has tremendous historic and religious significance not only for Judaism but for the whole world. He sees it as God's stake in human history, as the repudiation of despair, as a renewed call for trust in the Lord of history. Heschel argues that at its deepest roots Judaism is Zionist. He contends that modern political Zionism rides a millennial messianic wave of which its founders were only vaguely conscious.

The same view is enunciated by *Fisch* who argues that Israel's ideological identification with the Western liberalism tradition is rooted in a fallacy which has obscured the real spiritual and religious motives of Zionism. Fisch argues that a reformulation of the Jewish messianic myth is a key to understanding Israel's destiny. He detects a contemporary Zionist revolutionary movement which is concerned with a renewal of the bond with the land of Israel, and a revived sense of the Jewish people's and the State of Israel's unique roles in the world.

THE STATE AS SYMBOL OF PRESENT AND FUTURE HOPE

There are, however, Jews who refuse to apply the age-old yearning for Zion as expressed in the Liturgy to the creation and continuing existence of the State of Israel. Such a view is expressed by Reform *Rabbi Dow Marmur* who criticizes the way Israel is increasingly described in these terms when such description implies the blind application of Tradition.[60] This, Marmur contends, would be playing into the hands of the neo-Orthodox who want to interpret Judaism's future in terms of the dead past. This is a process which he labels "necrophilia." For Marmur it is vital that the interpretation of Israel is a matter for the present and the future and that it be seen as ushering in a new era of hope in the life of the Jewish people.

This view is given expression in the liturgy of Jewish Reform for the celebration of *Yom Ha'-atsma'ut* (Israel Independence Day). This is to be found in *The New Union Prayerbook* where there is a service for *Yom Ha-atsma-ut*[61] which was proclaimed as a permanent annual feast in the religious calendar of Reform Judaism.[62] The celebration recognizes that a new era has dawned in the life of the Jewish people. It attests the essential unity of the whole household of Israel and marks the cultural and spiritual renaissance which draws strength from the symbiotic relationship between Israel and diaspora Jewry. It sees the rebirth of Israel from the ashes of the Holocaust as a symbol of hope against despair, of redemption against devastation. There is, however, no attempt whatsoever in the service to link these realities with the messianic myth, even though Israel is clearly seen as an act of the Redeemer.

THE JEWISH HERMENEUTIC OF ISRAEL

Emerging from this investigation is the fact that there is no unified or typical Jewish understanding of Israel. For most Jews Israel is a Jewish "event." For some it is political, for others it is religious, and for still others it is both. For most it is associated with the two millennia of longing for Zion, and as such, for some, it is a political triumph, while for others it is a religious miracle and the answer to two millennia of prayer. For a great majority it is a focus of their Jewishness which some define in a religious way while others define it in a secular-cultural manner. For most Jews Israel is a metaphor of hope.

In sum, all interpretations converge on the *reality* of the State of Israel and all have a role in its hermeneutic. That hermeneutic is controlled not by any archetypal Zionist dogma, secular or religious, but by individual Jewish opinion which is influenced by a complexity of factors religious, political and cultural.

Since there is no means of prioritizing Jewish interpretations of Israel, be they political or religious or cultural, it must be concluded that all representative opinions may be considered valid expressions of contemporary Jewish thought about Israel, and that heterogeneity in the interpretation of Israel among contemporary Jews is simply a fact of Jewish existence.

THE PREDOMINANCE OF VITAL EXISTENTIAL ISSUES

The various Jewish ideological and hermeneutical issues are not of principal importance for Jews. Of paramount importance to them and of great urgency are the issues of contemporary Jewish existence.

Existential concerns have been predominant for Jews throughout the entire development of modern Zionism where it was focused on the problem of the *galut* (diaspora). The exile has always been viewed as an issue of Jewish existence and survival. It is intensively an existential issue for contemporary Jewry and contemporary Zionism now focused on questions arising from the events of the Holocaust and the foundation of the State of Israel. Survival and Identity are key issues for Jews, but they are also conundrums for contemporary Jewish history, philosophy, and theology.

A TIMELY CAUTION: THE DIALOGUE IS IN A STATE OF FLUX

The Jewish world-community in its internal dialogue is slowly awakening to the meaning of the events of its contemporary history. It simultaneously is becoming increasingly aware of the underlying existential issues. It is involved in a process which has as yet obviously not produced satisfactory answers and interpretations and which appears to have no foreseeable *terminus ad quem* when such results might become available.

It is because of this state of the internal dialogue that *H. Siegman* warns that Christians would be happier if they were allowed to deal with

Israel as a directly political phenomenon and that Jews should not draw them into the religious dimension, because

> Jews have hardly sorted out for themselves the meaning of the return of Jewish political sovereignty to the Land of Israel and the ways this miraculous phenomenon affects their lives and religious sensibilities. The development is too recent and too overwhelming for things to be otherwise.[63]

Rabbi A. Heschel informs us that there is no answer yet available to the question "What is the meaning of the State of Israel?" because Jews have not begun to fathom the meaning of this great event. They do not fully grasp its message for them, he claims, as a community and as individuals. As yet, he contends, it has not penetrated their capacity for representing its meaning in their daily lives.[64]

THE SITUATION: A SLOW JEWISH AWAKENING TO THE RELIGIOUS SIGNIFICANCE OF ISRAEL

In Chapter III the question was raised as to whether the vagueness of Jewish opinions on the religious significance of Israel, to be found in the reports in Chapter II, suggests that Jewish theology is in disarray on this subject. The evidence advanced in this chapter displays an agonizingly slow Jewish awakening to the meaning of Israel, religious or otherwise.

THE REALITY: THE STATE OF ISRAEL: A NEW FORM OF JEWISH EXISTENCE

In spite of the wide and varied nature of Jewish understandings about the State of Israel, it is nevertheless clear from the contemporary Jewish authors whose works have been consulted in this chapter that, for universal Jewry, whatever form it might take, the establishment of the State of Israel signals a new and precious form of Jewish existence in the contemporary world.

A WARNING ABOUT CONSULTING JEWISH LITERARY AND LITURGICAL SOURCES

In this study we have sought to examine the feasibility of using Jewish literary and liturgical texts as means by which to "listen" to the internal Jewish dialogue on Israel and thus come to an understanding of how Jews interpret Israel.

Literary Sources

The evidence which we have considered here would suggest that the use of Jewish literary sources as a tool by which to "listen" to the contemporary Jewish dialogue on Israel is very successful. However, it also indicates that the "listener" should not expect to find neat theological formulas which could be said to represent Jewish opinions, or hope to raise a Jewish consensus of interpretation, because neither is available.

Liturgical Sources

The suggestion that Jewish liturgical texts might provide a source for "listening" to the internal Jewish dialogue on Israel to discover how they interpret the State of Israel, in the presence of the evidence adduced in this chapter, is simply not sound.

Though the liturgy of the synagogue and the home is saturated with references to the messianic hope of the return of Jews to their ancient homeland, to the restoration of the nation, and to the establishment of the Lord's reign, consultation of these texts on a *lex orandi lex credendi* principle, which appears to be the basis of the suggestion, would be totally misleading for those who would seek what contemporary Jews understand about Israel.

Religious Jews themselves are, as we have seen, reluctant to make any application of the messianic hopes expressed in the liturgy to the return to the land and the rebirth of the nation-State. We have seen how Reform, in particular, has avoided doing this.

The fact that there has been no attempt by any sector of Judaism to alter the messianic expression of the liturgy to align it with the contemporary events of Jewish history is itself significant. It is a fact which parallels the state of the internal Jewish dialogue on Israel among religious Jews.

SIGNIFICANT NEW EVIDENCE TO CONSIDER

New and crucial evidence has emerged from our investigations in this chapter, which sheds light on the problem of Israel in the Catholic-Jewish dialogue.

First, there is the fact that Jews are undecided about the meaning of

Israel for themselves in spite of the fact that the *reality* of Israel is paramount for them.

Second, there is the fact that there exists in Jewry widely heterogeneous opinions about the meaning of Israel and the events surrounding its birth. Many of these opinions are mutually exclusive.

Third, underlying this state of flux in the internal Jewish dialogue on Israel there exists, beyond all its ideological endeavors, a fundamental search for the meaning of Jewishness and the purpose of Jewish existence in the contemporary world. The evidence adduced indicates that this search is a matter of great urgency for the worldwide Jewish community. This would account for the demands for existential rather than notional recognition, whether that be political, ontological or theological, or all of these recognitions, which we observed in the reports from Jewish leaders in Chapter II, and which was noted in Chapter III.

These are factors which have not been taken into consideration in the overview of the problem of Israel in the Catholic-Jewish dialogue. Their emergence together with the other evidence which we have uncovered in our study reveals a very different perspective on the putative theological problem.

In Chapter IV in this study the evolutionary process and the evolving attitude of the Catholic Magisterium toward the State of Israel was identified and recognized as a major reason for the Catholic Church's statement concerning Israel in *Notes*. In the same chapter the careful openness of the Catholic Church to Jewish sensibilities and understandings about Israel, through the documents of the Holy See, the papal allocutions, and the episcopal guidelines, was noted. It was identified as an openness which was seeking *"a slowly developing growth in understanding of what the return of Jews to the land and the rebirth of the nation-State of Israel means for contemporary Jews."*

It would appear from the evidence considered in this chapter that the slow awakening of the Catholic Church to the meaning of Israel is matched by a similar slow awakening to the meaning of Israel in the worldwide Jewish community.

However, for both, but more especially for the Catholic Church which is not, unlike Jews, involved in that internal dialogue on Israel, that slow awakening is confused by the cacophony of opinions about the meaning of Israel which are to be heard in the internal Jewish dialogue on that subject. This is a serious difficulty. It is a difficulty which also contributes to a refocused problem of Israel in the Catholic-Jewish dialogue. Yet it is a difficulty which has been overlooked by commentators on that dialogue. It would appear to be the major contributing factor of the continuing Catholic Magisterial prudent silence on Israel and its meaning for Jews.

A refocused view of the problem of Israel in the dialogue would require that all of this evidence be taken into consideration to modify further the perceived meaning of Magisterial prudence and silence on Israel. A refocused view would then perceive this silence as the "space" in which the Catholic Church's evolving and, with Jews, struggling understanding of the meaning of Israel for Jews is developing.

VIII.   Conclusion

The foregoing investigations of the problem of Israel in the Catholic-Jewish dialogue have revealed new evidence which gives a vastly different perspective to the problem.

REFOCUSING THE PROBLEM

The Problem Is Not of a Theological Nature

The evidence arising from this study indicates that there is no basis for the assertion that a fundamental theological difficulty experienced by the Catholic Church underlies the problem of Israel in the Catholic-Jewish dialogue. The evidence shows that there is no such problem.

The instruction in *Notes* at VI, 25 that:

> Christians are invited to understand this religious attachment [*to the land*] which finds its roots in biblical tradition without, however, making their own any particular religious interpretation of this relationship (cf. Declaration of the US Conference of Catholic Bishops, November 20, 1970).

> The existence of the State of Israel and its political options should be envisaged not in a perspective which is in itself religious, but in their reference to the common principles of international law,

in the light of the evidence adduced throughout this study, should not be interpreted as an indication of an underlying fundamental theological problem. There is simply no justification for interpreting this statement in that way. All the evidence produced above demonstrates the invalidity of such an assertion.

Neither should that statement be interpreted as the Catholic Church's refusal for all time to accept the Jewish theological challenge. It does not exclude the possibility that at some time in the future the Church might come to understand the theological meaning of Israel. It is clear, though, in the face of the heterogeneous nature of Jewish understandings, religious and otherwise, about Israel, that this statement is a warning to Catholics against, at this moment, in these circumstances, selecting any one particular interpretation as being the truth or even as being representative of Jewish opinion. For the present the authors of *Notes* instruct that "*The existence of the State of Israel and its political options should be envisaged not in a perspective which is itself religious, but in their reference to international law*" (VI, 25).

It is a great pity that the writers of this document had not made explicit their meaning in this instruction. It is obscurely indicated in the codicil "(*cf. Declaration of the U.S. Conference of Catholic Bishops, November 20, 1975*) (VI, 25)." Eugene Fisher as the Executive Secretary of the Secretariat for Catholic-Jewish Relations and one who is privy to the mind of the U.S. Conference of Catholic Bishops has informed us that this instruction and its codicil points to a reference in the 1975 document which focuses on fundamentalist religious interpretations applied to Israel in the U.S.A.[1] The problem with such interpretations, Fisher explains, is that they are ill-conceived and might also prove inimical to an eventual theological understanding of the meaning of Israel and of the events surrounding its rebirth.[2]

In circumstances where Jews themselves are so completely divided and confused in their own interpretations of the events of their recent history, which focus on the Holocaust and the creation of the State of Israel, it would be an act of patronizing impertinence for the Catholic Magisterium to assert a theological interpretation of Israel.

In any event, it is not the role of the Catholic Church to define theology for Jews. It is, however, always the duty of the Church to "watch" (Mark 13:33, 36, 37; Matthew 24:42, 43; 25:13, 38, 40; Luke 10:37, 39) and to keep herself alert to the "signs of the times." This activity is theological. In doing this the Church has implicitly accepted the Jewish theological challenge. In the developing tradition exemplified in the Magisterial teaching about Jews and Judaism, which was indicated in Chapter IV, there is abundant evidence of such theological activity.

We have noted its slow, ponderous, cautious progress. It is a profound theological activity but not a rapid one.

The Problem Is of a Complex Nature

The evidence which we have considered has revealed that the issue of Israel in the Catholic-Jewish dialogue is of an entirely different and much more complex nature than it has been judged at a superficial level.

ON THE JEWISH SIDE OF THE DIALOGUE

The Jewish contribution to the problem has been shown in Chapter VII to consist of three elements: the acephalous nature of Jewry, its inner pluriformity, and the heterogeneous nature of Jewish interpretations of the meaning of Israel.

These three elements indicate that there is little hope for a consensus of Jewish interpretation of Israel which non-Jews might identify as being *the* way in which Jews want them to understand Israel. The nature of the internal Jewish dialogue on Israel presents the Catholic partner in the dialogue with an insoluble dilemma in trying to discern "*by what essential traits the Jews define themselves in the light of their own religious experience.*"[3]

ON THE CATHOLIC SIDE OF THE DIALOGUE

The evidence which has emerged throughout this study indicates that there is a serious flaw in the Church's dialogical method. The Catholic Church contributes significantly to the problem in the dialogue by its failure to respond to Jewish existential insecurity which is associated with the continuing safety and security of the State of Israel. This is the case even in situations where Israel is thrust immediately to the attention of Church leadership.

It is clearly apparent that the immense change of heart and attitudes developed and demonstrated by the Catholic Church since the Second Vatican Council is lost to Jews while the Catholic Magisterium remains prudently silent about the State of Israel. What is an ordinary method of Magisterial operation is, as shown in the reports in Chapter II and elsewhere in this study, totally misunderstood by the Jewish world community. While silence and prudence are wisdom for the Catholic Church they are folly for the dialogue with the Jews, since so many Jews interpret them as being malevolent in character and intention. Such silence evokes from the corporate Jewish memory the most serious doubts about the Catholic Church.

The Problem Restated

In the chemistry of the Catholic-Jewish dialogue, Jewish existential insecurity with its focus on Israel and the prudent silence of the Catholic Magisterium on issues relating to Israel have amalgamated to produce the problem in the dialogue.

This problem is anchored in two facts. First, that after the Holocaust the Jewish civilization of Europe is no more. The center of that civilization has moved to its place of origin in Israel. The State of Israel is the new form of Jewish existence, and any threat to Israel represents a threat to Jewish existence itself. Second, that Catholic Magisterial silence on Israel is seen by Jews as calling into question the continuing existence of the State of Israel and, consequently, it is interpreted as a threat to Jewish existence itself.

The resulting problem is, as the evidence in the survey in Chapter II strongly indicates, that the dialogue between Catholics and Jews cannot exist indefinitely in its current state exacerbated by the fusion of Jewish insecurity and Catholic prudent silence, without drastic deterioration.

RECOMMENDATIONS FOR THE RESOLUTION OF THE PROBLEM

For the Jewish Partners in the Dialogue

There is an urgent need for Jewish partners in the theological dialogue with the Catholic Church to do two things. First, to objectively review and assess the official Catholic position on Israel within the total framework of its developments in relation to Jews and Judaism since the proceedings of the Second Vatican Council. Second, to study objectively the parameters of their own internal dialogue on Israel, attempting to assess its difficulties for non-Jews. Only by doing these things will Jews come to understand that the Catholic position on Israel as expressed in *Notes* VI, 25 and by the prudent silence of the Magisterium is not entrenched in a sinister pseudo-theology. Jews would then see that hermeneutical understanding of Israel is a very serious dilemma for the non-Jew and for the Catholic Church.

For the Catholic Partners in the Dialogue

The theological dialogue becomes a monologue when the subject of Israel appears on the agenda. The Catholic partner is mute. In these circumstances the Holy See's direction concerning *"real dialogue"* in *Guidelines (1974)* needs to be invoked. There we find the directive that *"such relations as there have been between Jews and Christians have scarcely ever risen above the level of monologue. From now on **real dialogue** (emphasis added) must be established."*

In *Guidelines (1974)* *"real dialogue"* is defined as *"mutual listening, mutual knowledge, mutual respect."* What is not explicit in this document is the criterion that *real dialogue* also requires from its partners an honest exchange and the desire to meet the other's needs and to respond to their demand for growth and affirmation.

It is these reciprocal ingredients in an otherwise *real dialogue* marked by mutual listening, knowledge and respect that are lacking from the official Catholic representation when Israel is raised by Jews.

Catholic partners in the official theological dialogue with Jews must understand that the wisdom of prudent silence on Israel, which is exercised by the Magisterium and by its individual spokespeople, is a totally inappropriate measure in the presence of Jewish existential anguish and insecurity relating to the State of Israel.

Catholic partners in the official dialogue must recognize that the various Jewish ideological and hermeneutical issues focusing on Israel which have been identified throughout this study are of secondary importance for Jews. They are symbolic of underlying and far more crucial issues of Jewish existence and survival in the contemporary world. What really matters for Jews who seek theological recognition for Israel from the Catholic Church is not the nature of the *theological* recognition but the nature of *recognition* itself. It must not be *notional* but a recognition of Jewry as a *living reality* and as *a people* who continue to struggle for their survival against hostile forces. They will understand that the State of Israel is the focus and symbol, the "incarnation" of this new contemporary Jewish existence. Furthermore, it must be understood that recognition of Israel is the litmus test by which Jews can gauge the degree of their existential safety in the contemporary world. It is *the* sign by which they are accepted as *a people*.

The Catholic Church must enjoin Jewish requests for existential recognition with Israel at its center. Such recognition would involve two stages.

First, there is need for an *official exchange* from Catholic Church leaders which would break the dialogical nexus created by the wisdom of prudent silence and the existential insecurity of contemporary Jews.

There is need for Jews to experience that even though the Catholic Church does not yet fully understand the presence and meaning of Israel, as Jews themselves do not, she does understand and shares and supports their deepest existential needs *as a people* for acceptance and security in the contemporary world all of which are symbolized by and focused in the State of Israel.

Such an action would not imply sanction of any decisions of the Israeli Government nor every action of the population of Israel. A great number of Jews themselves dissent on such matters. Criticism of the State of Israel, as of any state, is perfectly legitimate and necessary, from Jew and non-Jew, provided, as a matter of principle, that the right of the existence of that State is not being called into question.

Such action would require an open and honest exchange with Jews about Israel. The initiative for this is entirely with the Catholic partner of the official theological dialogue. From the Jewish side of the official dialogue it is already well in evidence as can be seen by the forthrightness of Jewish opinion in the reports in Chapter II.

A second stage, but one not contingent upon the first, would see developments toward the establishment of full de jure diplomatic relations between the Holy See and the State of Israel. This action would be the clear signal to Jews and to the rest of the world that the Holy See recognizes that Israel is an embodiment of Jewish identity, Jewish hopes and Jewish faith. The evidence presented in this study indicates the overwhelming necessity for this action. It is a necessity for justice and morality which far outweighs any inevitable opposition which would arise from Israel's enemies.

Both of these measures would advance the official dialogue between Catholics and Jews beyond the verbal to the stage of concrete action.

Appendix A: Addresses, Remarks and Homilies of Pope John Paul II, 1979–1986

The purpose of this survey is to indicate dates and places of Papal allocutions which relate to Jews and Judaism during the period 1979–1986.

The page references are to E. Fisher and L. Klenicki (eds.), *Pope John Paul II on Jews and Judaism, 1979–1986*. Where possible, cross-references are provided to alternative sources of these Papal allocutions.

1979

12 March   Audience for Representatives of Jewish Organizations (A response to Philip Klutznick, President of the World Jewish Congress), 21–23.

7 June   Homily at Auschwitz, 26–27.

3 October   To the Jewish Community, New York, 27.

1980

19 March   To a group from the British Council of Christians and Jews, at a General Audience in Rome, 29 (L'Osservatore Romano [Eng. ed.] 12 [625] March 24, 1980, 12).

31 May   At a meeting with the Jewish community in Paris, 29–30 (L'Osservatore Romano [Eng. ed.] 22 [635] June 2, 1980, 9).

3 July   Address to the Jewish Community at São Paulo, Bra-

zil, 30–31 (L'Osservatore Romano [Eng. ed.] 29 [642] July 21, 1980, 7).

5 October   Homily at the conclusion of a pilgrimage to Otranto, Italy, 31–33 (L'Osservatore Romano [Eng. ed.] 41 [653] October 13, 1980, 1, 2, 8).

17 November   Address to the Jewish Community at Mainz, West Germany, 33–36.

1982

6 March   Address to delegates to the meeting of representatives of Episcopal Conferences and other experts in Catholic-Jewish Relations: Commission for Religious Relations with Judaism, 37–40.

14 May   Address to religious leaders in Lisbon, Portugal, 40.

15 May   Address to religious leaders in Sameiro, Portugal, 40–42.

31 May   Address to the Jewish Community at Manchester, England, 42–44 (L'Osservatore Romano [Eng. ed.] 23 [737] June 7, 1982, 7).

1 June   Address to the Jewish Community, Scotland, 44–45.

3 November   Address to leaders of the Jewish Community, Madrid, Spain, 45.

1983

13 April   An address to a Jewish delegation on the fortieth anniversary of the Warsaw Gheto uprising, 47–48.

15 April   An address to the Catholics of France at Lourdes, 48–49.

10 September   An address at the "European Vespers" celebration, Vienna, Austria, 49–50 (L'Osservatore Romano [Eng. ed.] 38 [801] September 13, 1983, 3–4).

1984

22 March
An address to the Anti-Defamation League of B'nai B'rith at the Vatican, 51–52 (L'Osservatore Romano [Eng. ed.] 13 [827] March 26, 1984, 8).

20 April
The Apostolic Letter Redemptionis Anno, 55–57 (L'Osservatore Romano [Eng. ed.] 18 [832] April 30, 1984, 6–7).

14 June
An address to representatives of the Jewish community in Fribourg, Switzerland, 57–58 (L'Osservatore Romano 28 [842] July 9, 1984, 3).

6 July
An address to the Executive Committee of the International Council of Christians and Jews, at the Vatican, 60–62.

1985

15 February
An address to the American-Jewish Committee, in response to Howard Friedman, at the Vatican, 66–68 (The Pope Speaks, 30 2 [1985], 157–162).

19 April
A statement in response to the remarks of Rabbi B. Sobel at a colloquium on Nostra Aetate at the Angelicum in Rome, 70–73.

28 October
An address to the International Catholic-Jewish Liaison Committee on the twentieth anniversary of Nostra Aetate, Rome, 74–76.

1986

13 April
An address at the Pope's visit to the Synagogue of Rome, 79–85 (The Pope Speaks 31 3 [1986], 193–198).

5 June
Remarks at a General Audience in St. Peter's Square, Rome, 92.

6 November   Response to a statement by Nathan Perlmutter at a conference at the Angelicum, Rome, 93.

26 November   An Address to the Jewish Community in Australia, 95–97 (L'Osservatore Romano [Eng. ed.] 48 [965] December 1, 1986).

Appendix B: Guidelines of Particular Churches, from 1967

The purpose of this survey is to make the contents of the various guidelines, in summarized form, immediately available to the reader. It also serves to demonstrate how universally and deeply the Catholic Church has responded to the initiatives of *Nostra Aetate* and *Guidelines (1974)*.

A critical evaluation of these guidelines is provided by Sister Charlotte Klein, N.D.S. in *Christian-Jewish Relations* 17 1 (1984), 32–36.

A concise and useful table of events relating to the publication of the various guidelines and pastoral letters for the period 1965–1975 is provided by the editors, *SIDIC* VIII, 3 (1975), 13–20.

1967. **USA GUIDELINES FOR CATHOLIC-JEWISH RELATIONS** (published by the American Bishops' Sub-Committee for Catholic-Jewish Relations).

SIDIC III, 2 (1970), 10–16.

■

Rome, LOST GUIDELINES
These were drawn up by some American Bishops. They were never promulgated but disappeared in the Vatican archives, though their contents were elaborated by the official Vatican Secretariat for Catholic-Jewish Relations which included several Bishops. They stress the following:

(i)   the election of the Jewish people;

(ii) that all attempts at conversion are to be abandoned;

(iii) the link between Israel's Covenant and the Land;

(iv) the return of the Jewish People to the promised land as quite legitimate;

(v)   the need to seek the Jewish people's forgiveness for former persecutions.

H. Croner (ed.), *Stepping Stones To Further Jewish-Christian Relations,* **6–11.**

SIDIC III (1970), 2.

(See **C. Klein, Christian–Jewish Relations 17, 1, 1984, 30–31,** for her comments on these "Lost Guidelines.")

■

1970. **Vienna, DIRECTIVES REGARDING JEWISH-CHRISTIAN RE-LATIONS** (published by the Synod of the Diocese of Vienna).

SIDIC IV, 2 (1970), 42.

■

1970. **Netherlands, PASTORAL RECOMMENDATIONS ON RELA-TIONS BETWEEN JEWS AND CATHOLICS** (published by the Pastoral Council of the Catholic Church in the Netherlands).

SIDIC III, 2 (1970), 25–32.

■

1973. **France, PASTORAL ORIENTATIONS ON THE ATTITUDE OF CHRISTIANS TO JUDAISM** (published by the Episcopal Committee of the Bishops of France).

This document is more theological than most others. It asserts that Jesus "renewed" the Covenant of God with Israel and extended it. It affirms that the Jewish election continues, as well as a definite Jewish vocation in the world, "a sanctification of the Name." There are a number of biblical references to prove that the land of Israel is God's permanent gift to the Jewish people, though a just solution of the Arab problem is also called for. Both Jews and Christians have the right to bear witness to their faith but without any attempt at proselytizing. Israel and the Church will co-exist until the end of time: a sign that the divine plan for humankind is not yet complete.

SIDIC VI, 2 (1973), 30–33.

SIDIC VI, 3 (1973), 38–41.

■

1975. **Galveston (USA), GUIDELINES** (published by the Archdiocese of Galveston, Houston). This document deals with the following areas.

1. Antisemitism. 2. The Holocaust. 3. The State of Israel. (This is a statement which attempts to establish a balance between Arab and Jewish rights and feelings, while clearly recognizing the religious and historic longing Jews have had for a nation and a land of their own, a longing reinforced by the Holocaust. It recognizes the existence of the State of Israel, along with the right which other Middle Eastern nations have to existence. It states that such recognition of these nations does not necessarily imply an endorsement of every political activity and position of their respective governments.) 4. Comparison and continuity of the Jewish and Christian traditions. 5. Prayer and worship. 6. The need for dialogue with the Jewish community. 7. The liturgical pattern. 8. Responsibility for the death of Jesus. 9. Intermarriage. 10. Religion in the Jewish community. 11. Cooperation in social action. 12. Being a pilgrim in the world.

H. Croner (ed.), *More Stepping Stones,* **74–78.**

■

1975. **USA Bishops' Conference, Pastoral Letter** (published by the Secretariat for Catholic-Jewish Relations, Bishops' Committee on Ecumenical and Interreligious Affairs, National Conference of Catholic Bishops). Sets out general principles and recommended programs. The text was prepared in conjunction with the tenth anniversary of *Nostra Aetate,* and in it the Bishops reflect on the development in Jewish-Church relationships since 1965.

Christian Attitudes on Jews and Judaism 47, April (1976), 13–16. Also in SIDIC VIII, 3 (1975), 36–39.

■

1977. **USA LOS ANGELES** (published by the Archdiocese of Los Angeles). This speaks of the long and deep sense of mutual respect between the Church and the Jewish Community. It advises that Catholics in dialogue with Jews should acknowledge the following sensitivities and growing concerns. 1. The Holocaust. 2. The State of Israel. 3. Antisemitism. 4. Proselytizing. 5. Interfaith marriage. All of these things, it maintains, though not intended to be all-inclusive, are agenda concerns, and Catholics should be aware that these issues will influence all dialogue in which the Jewish Community becomes involved. The document also treats of I) Local Dialogues; different natures and forms of dialogue; II) Catholic-Jewish Marriages.

SIDIC XI, 1 1978, 24–26.

■

1979. **USA, LOUISVILLE (Seder Guidelines. A Joint Statement of Archdiocesan Offices, Archdiocese of Louisville).** It addresses parishes which celebrate the Seder Meal, encouraging them to deepen their knowledge of Jewish rituals. Seder is to be seen in the context of contemporary Judaism, not as something surpassed by the Eucharist. Catholics are encouraged to seek Jewish help for the celebration and should not attempt to create links between the Seder and the Last Supper. Catholics must maintain the integrity of the Jewish ritual.

H. Croner (ed.), *More Stepping Stones,* **79.**

■

1979. **Germany, Bonn (Basic Theological Issues of the Jewish-Christian Dialogue;** this arises from a workshop of Jews and Christians and is published by the Central Committee of Roman Catholics in Germany). This document explores the question "Why seek the Dialogue?" It also deals with conditions of the Dialogue which concern Jew as Jew and Christian as Christian, and the central themes of the Dialogue. The text seeks to bring about an awareness that the Jewish-Christian Dialogue must no longer remain the monopoly of the few interested specialists. It urges Christians to devote themselves to the central topics of the Dialogue, and to bring these topics to public attention.

H. Croner (ed.), *More Stepping Stones*, 111–119.

■

1979. USA, Brooklyn, Catholic-Jewish Relations—Guidelines (published by the Diocese of Brooklyn).

Attempts to address the meaning and purpose of interreligious dialogue with reference to *Nostra Aetate*. Speaks about the nature of dialogue; the responsibility to be involved in the dialogue; the duty of the Church to foster unity and charity among individuals, and mutual understanding between religious traditions. 1. Lists Catholic concerns, areas of special sensitivity. 2. Lists areas of special sensitivity for the Jewish Community, among these the State of Israel, noting the great pride American Jews have in that State and its accomplishments, and especially in the new life Israel has made possible for the survivors of the Holocaust and for Jews who have escaped from the Soviet Union. It acknowledges that to many Jews the establishment of the State of Israel represents the fulfillment of divine promises in Scripture. 3. Surveys opportunities for dialogue.

H. Croner (ed.), *More Stepping Stones*, 87–91.

■

1979. USA, CLEVELAND, GUIDELINES (published by the Diocese of Cleveland). These Guidelines stress that the great benefit of interfaith dialogue has been the appreciation by the Church of its unique relationship to the Jewish people and the Jewish religion. They claim that the roots of the Church are in God's revelation to Israel on Sinai and that the Church considers herself as sharing in Israel's election, in Christ. Therefore, it is asserted that Christians should enter into dialogue with

Jews with more than good will. Christian respect and regard for Judaism is not as for some ancient relic of the past. God made Jews his own and gave them an irrevocable vocation. Catholics must genuinely repent of all forms of antisemitism. All people in any form of leadership in the Church must work to counter any such attitudes, even the most subtle expressions. The authors then list ten specific points of importance, and among them the sensitive and very deeply rooted feelings which Jewish people have toward the State of Israel. Catholics are alerted that they should also seek to be correctly informed about the complex political differences between Arabs and the people of Israel.

H. Croner (ed.), *More Stepping Stones,* **85–86.**

■

1979. **USA, Detroit, GUIDELINES** (published by the Ecumenical Commission of the Archdiocese of Detroit). The document is divided into three sections. 1. Attitudes inconsistent with the spirit of Christ: clichés and stereotypes from the past; blame for Jesus' death; the claim that the Jewish people have been deprived of their election. 2. The right understanding of Judaism: the permanence of the Covenant; the permanent vocation of the Jewish people; Jewish Law as gestures reminding people of the sovereignty of God; the right of both Jews and Christians to give full witness to their faith; the dispersion of the Jewish people and their in-gathering, which is to be seen in the light of Jewish history and Jewish perspectives. Calls Catholics to be sensitive to the deeply held American Jewish sensitivity for the State of Israel. Recognizes the right of Israel to exist, and also the right of the Palestinian peoples. 3. Practical guidelines: for prayer; social action; reconciliation; liturgy; education.

H. Croner (ed.), *More Stepping Stones,* **87–89.**

■

1980. **USA, NEW JERSEY, GUIDELINES FOR ECUMENICAL AND JEWISH-CATHOLIC RELATIONS** (published by the Diocese of Trenton, New Jersey). This document provides very practical guidelines which have obviously arisen from immediate pastoral needs. It looks specifically at the delicate problem of mixed marriages (Jewish-Catholic), attempting to handle the issue with tact and respect for the religious convictions of the Jewish partner. Some of the areas dealt with include: possible courses of action to promote understanding; worship in common; spiritual care; marriages; the wedding ceremony; the children; pastoral care and follow-up.

H. Croner (ed.), *More Stepping Stones*, 92–101.

■

1980. ENGLAND AND WALES, PASTORAL GUIDELINES (FOR PRIESTS, RELIGIOUS AND LAY PEOPLE)

Makes explicit reference to *Nostra Aetate* as its starting point, then moves to offer practical application of the key passages of *Guidelines* (*1974*): strong personal contact; house discussion groups; informal study groups; mutual visits; awareness in the classroom. Raises the issue of sharing in common prayer and meditation, calling for spiritual sensitivity. Sees the pulpit as a powerful platform for combating antisemitism, especially in Holy Week. It encourages priests to stress the spiritual and historical links which bind the Church and Judaism. Sees the dialogue as working together for the good of all peoples, building up a more just, humane and peaceful society. It encourages invitations to local Jewish leaders to attend parochial action meetings at which important economic, social, cultural and political issues are discussed. It wants Catholics to see that Jews and Christians belong to the family of the people of God; that in God's design the family is basically one. Outlines essential requirements for fruitful dialogue: the practice of prayer, a deep commitment to faith, honesty and truthfulness, love of God and of others.

H. Croner (ed.), *More Stepping Stones*, 120–123.

■

1980. GERMANY (BONN), THE CHURCH AND THE JEWS: GERMAN BISHOPS' CONFERENCE.

This long and comprehensive document is divided into six sections: 1. Jesus Christ; 2. Israel's spiritual heritage; 3. the testimony of Scripture and the Church concerning the relationship between the Church and Judaism; 4. differences of belief; 5. changes of attitudes toward Judaism; 6. common ground.

Christian-Jewish Relations **73, Dec. 1980, 25–42. Also available in H. Croner (ed.),** *More Stepping Stones,* **124–131.**

■

1982. **AUSTRIA, GUIDELINES.**

1. Clarify in some detail the common heritage of Judaism and Christianity. 2. Speak out against the latest form of antisemitism: anti-Zionism. 3. Attempt to redefine the role of the Pharisees in the Christian Scriptures, and the term "the Jews" in the Gospel of John. 4. Give a brief historical survey of the fate of Jews in Christian society. 5. Distinguish between old religious antisemitism and modern racial-biological antisemitism which led to the Holocaust.

SIDIC XIV, 1 (1983), 24–26

■

1983. **USA, GUIDELINES FOR JEWISH-CATHOLIC MARRIAGES, ARCHDIOCESE OF NEWARK.**

These guidelines arise from pastoral practice: mixed marriages between Catholics and Jews. They are addressed to priests and deacons. They deal with: 1. pastoral concerns; 2. preparation for marriage; 3. the wedding ceremony. They contain appendices with (a) reflections on Catholic-Jewish marriage and (b) remarks to the Jewish Catholic couple.

H. Croner (ed.), *More Stepping Stones,* **102–108.**

■

1983. **ROME, ECUMENICAL GUIDELINES: DIOCESE OF ROME.**

Emphasizing different ways of developing an ecumenical mentality in the faithful of the Diocese of Rome. Devotes a section to relations with Jews, in the context of a search for a wider reconciliation which embraces the whole people of God. Beginning with a response to *Nostra Aetate,* the document encourages and promotes relationships, setting out some guidelines. It stresses that those involved in dialogue must learn how Jews define themselves in the light of their own religious experience. It attests to the content and language used in different pastoral situations in order to avoid explicit or implicit antisemitism. It encourages Catholics to rediscover and give value to Jewish roots in Catholic liturgy. It urges the development of initiatives—meetings, conferences, publications, etc.—to help Christians to increase their knowledge of Judaism. It encourages Jews and Christians to read the Hebrew Scriptures together. It encourages Catholics toward a knowledge of Jewish liturgical life, and Jews and Catholics to a common commitment to a more human and fraternal life-style in the City of Rome. It proposes an objective collaboration between the Jewish community and the parish community; it deals with mixed marriages and their pastoral care.

H. Croner (ed.), *More Stepping Stones,* **146–148.**

■

1984. **BRAZIL, ORIENTATIONS FOR CATHOLIC JEWISH DIALOGUE.** NATIONAL COMMISSION FOR CATHOLIC-JEWISH RELATIONS DIALOGUE: NATIONAL CONFERENCE OF BRAZILIAN BISHOPS.

A brief to-the-point document reiterating the teaching and sentiments of both *Nostra Aetate* and *Guidelines (1974)*. Treats of: the need for dialogue; the singularity of Judaism and its monotheistic faith; the divine election and constitution of Israel. Judaism's permanent witness and vocation. The condemnation of all forms of antisemitism; the unfavorable Catholic teaching about Jews and Judaism of the past. On not contrasting Judaism with Christianity; the Jewish roots of Christianity. The document also comments positively on the land of Israel and the rights of Jews to a calm political existence in "the country of their origin," without letting that create injustice or violence to other people. It states that "for the Jewish people their right became a reality in the State of Israel." Finally, the document emphasizes the eschatological expectation which is the hope of Jews and Christians, despite their different ways of interpretation. It is in this eschatological awareness that both paths converge: both Christians and Jews are in search of a land "flowing with milk and honey."

H. Croner (ed.), *More Stepping Stones,* **151–153.**

■

1985. **USA, GUIDELINES FOR CATHOLIC-JEWISH RELATIONS.**
NATIONAL CONFERENCE OF CATHOLIC BISHOPS. SECRE-
TARIAT FOR CATHOLIC-JEWISH RELATIONS.

This document is a revision of the 1967 and 1975 documents. Opening
with a reference to *Nostra Aetate,* it proceeds to discuss the dialogical
encounter with Jews, its origin, purpose, nature and progress. It focuses
on the positive direction which Pope John Paul II has sought to give to
the dialogue, and on the unique opportunities which the Church in the
U.S.A. has for dialogue with Jews. The document sets out nine General
Principles and eleven recommended programs. (1) A commission or
secretariat for each diocese. (2) That Catholics should take initiative in
fostering Catholic-Jewish understanding. (3) The general aim of meetings: to increase mutual understanding. (4) The genuine respect which
must exist in the dialogue. (5) The use of expertise to facilitate fruitful
dialogue. (6) Mutual witness without proselytism. (7) The encouragement to engage in common prayer. (8) The acknowledgement of difficulties in mixed marriages. (9) The Holocaust and the State of Israel, and
the difficulty of sharing Jewish views on the latter, especially regarding
contemporary political controversies.

National Conference of Catholic Bishops, *Guidelines for Catholic Jewish*
Dialogue. **Washington: U.S. Catholic Conference, 1985.**

Notes

I. INTRODUCTION

1. Commission for Religious Relations with the Jews, *Notes on the correct way to present the Jews and Judaism in preaching and catechesis in the Roman Catholic Church* (June 24, 1985), VI, 25.

2. C. Klein, *The Theological Dimensions of the State of Israel,* Journal of Ecumenical Studies 10, 4 (1971), 700–715.

3. C.A. Rijk, *Recent Developments. SIDIC Study Session: People-Land-Religion,* SIDIC VIII, 2 (1975), 36–37.

4. C. Angell, *Jews and Catholics Since "Nostra Aetate,"* Christian Attitudes on Jews and Judaism, 46, February (1976), 10–14.

5. T. Stransky, *The Catholic-Jewish Dialogue: Twenty Years After "Nostra Aetate,"* America 154, February 8 (1986), 96.

6. E. Fisher, *The Holy See and the State of Israel: The Evolution of Attitudes and Policies,* Journal of Ecumenical Studies 24, 2 September (1987), 191–211.

7. Ibid. 202.

8. B. Williams, *Redemption and Morality in the Light of the Jewish-Catholic Dialogue,* Face to Face XIV, Spring (1988), 31–35.

9. G. Wigoder, Jewish-Christian Relations Since the Second World War (Manchester: Manchester University Press, 1988), 104–122, has written a chapter in which he attempts to summarize the problem of Israel in the dialogue in the broad Christian perspective.

10. The initiative for the renewal of Catholic relations with the Jews is attributed to Pope John XXIII. J. Oesterreicher believes that Pope John's motivation was strongly influenced by his conversations with Jules Isaac. See H. Vorgrimler, Commentary on the Documents of Vatican II (London: Burns & Oates, 1967), Volume III, 4. See also R.J. Werblowsky, *Broad-Minded Narrow-Mindedness,* Christian Jewish Relations 14, 4, 77 (1981), 37; and also E. Fisher, Faith Without Prejudice (New York: Paulist Press, 1980), 3–7. Augustine Bea, The Church and the Jewish People (London: Chapman, 1966), 22, the Cardinal Secretary for Christian Unity in 1960, recalls that *"Pope John XXIII received me in audience on 18 September 1960 and charged the Secretariat for Christian Unity with the task*

of preparing a Declaration dealing with the Jewish people. In doing so he took a second more decisive step along the road which opened up on Good Friday, 1959. It was on that day, during the solemn liturgy, that he had read out the order to omit the adjective 'perfidious' from the customary prayer for the Jews."

11. T. Stransky, *Focusing on Jewish-Catholic Relations,* Origins 15, 5 June (1985), 67.

12. Vatican Commission for Religious Relations with the Jews, Guidelines and Suggestions for Implementing the Conciliar Declaration "Nostra Aetate" (no. 4) (December 1, 1974), 1, "On Dialogue."

13. Ibid. Preamble.

14. Ref. H. Fisch, The Zionist Revolution (New York: St. Martin's, 1978), 4–7.

15. Ref. J. Parkes, The History of the Jewish People (Harmondsworth: Penguin, 1964) 41–44, to J. Neusner, Invitation to the Talmud (San Francisco: Harper and Row, 1984), 34–37.

II. THE PROBLEM FOR JEWS:
DEFINING JEWS IN CHRISTIAN PERSPECTIVES

1. Ref. E. Fisher, *Vatican Guidelines: Reactions around the World,* SIDIC VIII, 2 (1975), 37–41.

2. M. Jais, *On the Jewish-Christian Dialogue,* SIDIC VIII, 3 (1975), 27.

3. See D.G. Singer, *American Catholic Attitudes Towards the Zionist Movement and the Jewish State as Reflected in the Pages of "America," "Commonweal," and the "Catholic World," 1945–1976,* Journal of Ecumenical Studies 22, 4 (Fall 1983), 715–740.

4. Commission for Religious Relations with the Jews, Notes on the correct way to present the Jews and Judaism in preaching and catechesis in the Roman Catholic Church (June 24, 1985), IV, 25.

5. R. Apple, *An Open Letter to the Pope,* National Outlook, reprinted in Australia/Israel Review, 11, 21, 18 November–1 December (1986), 8.

6. *Jewish Criticism of Vatican Document,* The Tablet, 238, 6 July (1985), 709.

7. *Christianity and Judaism: The Unfinished Agenda,* Christian Jewish Relations, 19, 1 (1986), 57–63. In 1976, Siegman wrote an article critical of the Catholic Church for its silence on the State of Israel in which he said, ". . . *the failure of the Vatican guidelines to deal with the theological dimension of the Jewish relationship to the land of Israel constitutes a serious omission (. . .) it is impossible to understand Jews nor can anyone communicate meaningfully with them about their deepest fears or aspirations without an appreciation of the role of the State of Israel in Jewish consciousness.* Ref. Encounter Today XI, 2–3 (1976), 83. This statement explains the remark which is reported above.

8. E. Fisher and L. Klenicki (eds.), Pope John Paul II on Jews and Judaism, 1979–1986 (Washington: NCCB, 1987), 63–66.

9. Ibid. 76–78.
10. Ibid. 85–88.
11. Ibid. 88–91.
12. *Vatican Recognition of Israel,* The Tablet 238, 6 July (1985), 709.
13. The Tablet 241, 27 June (1988), 700.
14. A. Hertzberg, *Rome Must Recognize Israel,* Christian Jewish Relations, 19, 1 (1986), 50–52.
15. R. Wilikovsky, *Vatican Recognition of Israel,* The Tablet, 238, 6 July (1985), 72.
16. Idem.
17. Le Devoir, 26 February (1985), 6. Reprinted in SIDIC VIII, 2 (1985), 39.
18. Christian Jewish Relations, 18, 3 (1985), 21–23.
19. Ibid. 67–73.
20. Ibid. 42–43.
21. Ibid. 17–31.
22. Guidelines (1974), Preamble.

III. THE PROBLEM OF ANTISEMITISM—AND A SOLUTION

1. See H. Siegman, Christian Jewish Relations, 19, 1 (1986), 58. Compare his statement here with that in *Ten Years of Catholic-Jewish Dialogue: A Reassessment,* J. Willebrands (ed.), Fifteen Years of Catholic-Jewish Dialogue 1970–1985 (Vatican: Libreria Editrice, 1988), 29–33. See also A. Hertzberg, Christian Jewish Relations, 18, 3 (1985), 22.

2. Documentary evidence of this teaching is available in J. Isaacs, The Teaching of Contempt (New York: Holt, Reinhart & Winston, 1964), where he demonstrates that the Church in its teaching and legislation had ensured the humiliation of the Jews and brought up generation after generation to despise them. Isaacs identifies and elaborates on three main themes in the Church's teaching of contempt, the first of which is "*The Dispersion of the Jews as a Providential Punishment for the Crucifixion,*" pp. 39–68. Here Isaacs provides many examples of this teaching throughout the history of Christianity into the present era.

3. For example, see D. Prince (n.a.: Derek Prince Publications, 1981), especially pp. 47–56, *Why Do the Jews Suffer?* Also, see Australia/Israel Review, 7, 10, October 29–November 11 (1982), 8, where comments of the Anglican Dean of Perth, the Very Rev. David Robarts, are recorded ("*It was Jewish self-interest and false messianism that crucified Christ*"; "*Christians have no commitment to an Old Testament genocidal god . . .*"; "*The vast majority of Israeli Jews are settlers of non-semitic origins,*" etc.). Refer also to *The Dean and the Jews,* Australia/Israel Review, 8, 21, 10 November–23 November (1983), 8, where Rabbi Dr. John Levi exposes the Dean's anti-Zionist and antisemitic exploits, and his inaccurate knowledge. Refer also to Sr. Charlotte Klein, N.D.S., "*Anti-*

Judaism in a German Missal," Christian Jewish Relations, 17, 2 (1984), 48–50, who writes about the attitudes derivative from this pseudo-theology which are to be found in the Volks-Schott Missal (February 1975) where the introductory and explanatory notes for the readings of "Year B" frequently express anti-Jewish prejudice.

4. Civiltà Cattolica, X, 1 May (1897), 257–270 (reproduced by C. Klein, *The Theological Dimensions of the State of Israel,* Journal of Ecumenical Studies, 10, 4 [1973], 703).

5. M. Lowenthal (ed.), The Diaries of Theodor Herzl (London: Jewish Publication Society, 1958), 426.

6. Idem.

7. Civiltà Cattolica, 3, 15 July (1922), 118. Reprinted in C. Klein, art. cit. 704.

8. Quoted by C. Klein, ibid. 704–705.

9. A. Bea, The Church and the Jewish People (London: Chapman, 1966), 81–86.

10. W.M. Abbott, The Documents of Vatican II (London: Chapman, 1966), 660–668, *Declaration on the Relationship of the Church to Non-Christian Religions,* 4.

11. Ibid. 14–16, *Dogmatic Constitution on the Church,* 16.

12. J. Willebrands, op. cit. 301–303, *Address to Jewish Representatives, Mainz* (November 17, 1980).

13. E. Fisher and L. Klenicki (eds.), Pope John Paul II on Jews and Judaism 1979–1986 (Washington: NCCB, 1987), 38, *To delegates to the meeting of representatives of Episcopal Conferences and other experts in Christian-Jewish Relations: Commission for Religious Relations with Judaism* (March 3, 1982).

14. Ibid. 52, *To the Anti-Defamation League of B'nai B'rith* (22 March 1984).

15. Ibid. 96. *To the Jewish Community of Australia* (26 November 1986).

16. M. Jais, SIDIC VIII, 3 (1975), 27. See also G. Wigoder, Jewish-Christian Relations Since the Second World War (Manchester: Manchester University Press, 1988), 117, and also, from a Christian commentator: J.P. Lichtenberg, From the First to the Last of the Just (Israel: Ecumenical Theological Research Fraternity, 1979), 73.

17. The Tablet, 27 July (1985), 769–770.

18. Not all Catholics, however, were silent. J. Oesterreicher and E. Flannery wrote their statements of conscience (November 17, 1967). See SIDIC VIII, 2–3 (1968), 91–95.

19. R. Hochhuth, The Deputy (New York: Grove Press, 1964). Tr. R. and C. Winston.

20. J. Mejia, *The Catholic Style: A Reflection on the Documents,* H. Croner (ed.), More Stepping Stones to Jewish-Christian Relations (New York: Paulist, A Stimulus Book, 1985), 5–6.

21. The Jerusalem Post, 4 August 1988, 22.

22. In particular, see the reference to the State of Israel in the Apostolic Letter Redemptionis Anno (1984).

23. A. Hertzberg, Christian Jewish Relations 18, 3 (1985), 23; G. Riegner, *Twenty Years of Nostra Aetate,* Christian Jewish Relations, 18, 4 (1985), 27.

24. M. Mendes, *The Catholic Church, Judaism and the State of Israel,* Christian Jewish Relations, 21, 2 (1988), 27; E. Rackman, Christian Jewish Relations, 18, 3 (1985), 45; H. Siegman, Christian Jewish Relations, 19, 1 (1986), 60–62.

25. Cf. the comments of E. Fisher and L. Klenicki, op. cit., 17, 31–33. See also Paul VI, Nobis in Animo (1974), which is concerned with the security and survival of the Christian community in the Holy Land.

26. Cf. Fisher and Klenicki, op. cit., 17, and also A. Hertzberg, Christian Jewish Relations, 19, 1 (1986), 50–52.

27. Cf. J. Oesterreicher, Christian Jewish Relations, 19, 1 (1986), 52–53.

28. New York Times, 30 December (1985), 32. Reproduced in Christian Jewish Relations, 19, 1 (1986), 53–54.

29. J. Oesterreicher, art. cit. 52–53.

30. This concern of the Holy See is documented over a long period of time. Pius XII, Auspicia Quaedam (May 10, 1948), expresses "new anxiety" for the safety of the Holy Places, speaks about the international character of Jerusalem (October 24, 1948), and calls for international status for that city (April 15, 1949). Paul VI (December 23, 1968) calls for an internationally generated regulation on the question of Jerusalem and the Holy Places, and for an internationally legal safeguard for the city's Holy Places and religiously diverse population (June 24, 1971). In Nobis in Animo (March 25, 1974), the Pope speaks of the *"increased need of the Church in the Holy Land"*; the ancientness of the Christian tradition of pilgrimage; for care for pilgrims and Holy Places and for the continued survival of the Christian community.

31. See, for instance, Rabbi Brian Fox, Australia/Israel Review 10, 16, 3–18 September (1985), 1, who cites the published speech of Pope John Paul II in Osservatore Romano (22/08/85), "*. . . the Moslems are convinced that Jerusalem, being the capital city of the three monotheistic religions, should have special status.*" Fox claims that the Pope's comment "*. . . may have been highlighted by elements in the Vatican Secretariat of State who are not sympathetic to Israel.*" Fox asks: "*What can such a statement mean in the light of the Apostolic Letter 'Redemptionis Anno' which was devoted to Jerusalem?*"

32. For example, the event of the seizure of the Greek Orthodox hostel in the Old City at Easter 1990. This was the action of a fanatical fringe group known as the Ne'ot David, an offshoot of the Ateret Kohanim Yeshiva, a religious academy of fundamentalist Jews dedicated to the rebuilding of the Temple in Jerusalem. This group had made a dubious deal with the protected tenant of this very large building. The action was reversed by Israeli law.

33. See Ministry of Tourism, Pilgrim and Christian Tourist Promotion Handbook (Jerusalem: Ministry of Tourism, 1987), second edition.

34. The Declaration on Relations Between the Holy See and the State of Israel. Press Office to the Holy See, Vatican City, January 25, 1991.

35. Cf. Fisher and Klenicki, op. cit. 17.

36. E. Fisher, Christian Jewish Relations 18, 4 (1985), 57.

37. J. Maritain, Antisemitism (New York: Longman Green, 1939), 20.

38. E. Flannery, The Anguish of the Jews (New York: Paulist, A Stimulus Book 1985), 267–269.

39. R. Eckardt, *Antisemitism Is the Heart,* Christian Jewish Relations, 17, 4 (1984), 43–51, et passim.

40. For instance, see the reported statement of Pope John Paul II, The Tablet 19, August (1989), 954, where he is claimed to have used terminology which was considered to be unavoidably prejudicial, and which appears to contradict Magisterial teaching.

41. Nostra Aetate, IV.

42. Guidelines (1974), Preamble I, para. 6.

43. Notes, 26.

44. Fisher and Klenicki (eds), op. cit., *Audience for Representatives of Jewish Organizations* (12 March 1979).

45. Fisher and Klenicki, op. cit. 75, *Address to International Catholic-Jewish organizations* (12 March 1979).

46. SIDIC XXI 1 (1988), 27–30.

47. Pontifical Commission "Justitia et Pax," The Church and Racism (Homebush: St. Paul Publications, 1989), 32–33.

48. Cf. E. Fisher and L. Klenicki (eds.), Pope John Paul II on Jews and Judaism 1979–1986, 97.

49. Cf. the World Zionist Organization, Anti-Zionism: A Threat to Israel the Jewish People Democracy (Jerusalem: W.Z.O., n.a.), 3–4. In this publication is to be found a definition of anti-Zionism and an exposition of its many manifestations in contemporary society.

50. For instance, see W. Laqueur and B. Rubin (eds.), The Israeli-Arab Reader (London: Penguin, 1985): (1) The Record of Conversation between Hitler and the Grand Mufti of Jerusalem (28 November 1941), 80–84; (2) The Arab Case for Palestine (March 1946), 94–103; (3) Erskine Childer's "The Other Exodus," 143–151.

51. Cf. Flannery, op. cit. 268.

52. We should note that "*70 A.D.*" is the wrong date. It should be 135 A.D. This inaccuracy gives the impression that Judaism is only a religion, and that it somehow ends at the destruction of the Temple in 70 C.E.

53. Notes, 25.

54. Idem.

55. For instance, see the following documents in Laqueur and Rubin, The Israel-Arab Reader (London: Penguin, 1985): 131–134, The Draft Constitution of the Palestinian Liberation Organisation; 167–168, F. A. Sayegh, Zionist Colo-

nization in Palestine; 169–174, G. Naser's Speech to the United Arab Republic (25/05/1967); 366–372, The Palestinian National Charter: Resolutions of the Palestinian National Council; 379–383, Platform of the Popular Front for the Liberation of Palestine; 504–518, Address of Yasir Arafat to the United Nations General Assembly (13/11/1977); 602–608, Arab League Summit Conference Declaration (5/12/1977); 686–691, Jordan's refusal to join the Reagan Peace Initiative (10/04/83).

56. Holy Land, Fall (1988), 151, a report by Greg Erlandson of N.C. News Service.

57. Notes, 25.

58. Pope John Paul II, Redemptionis Anno (1984). Cf. E. Fisher, *The Pope and Israel*, Christian Jewish Relations, 18, 1 (1985), 52–55.

59. Notes, 25.

60. In a critique of Pope John Paul II's Address at the Synagogue of Rome, Charles Krauthammer writes, "*The Pope addressed the wrong problem because he implicitly took the view that Jews are exclusively a religious community. Jews have never thought so. They have always considered themselves as a people. To address Jews purely as a religious community is to deny their peoplehood. The Pope obviously does so without malice*" (reported in the Australia/Israel Review 11, 6, 22 April–5 May [1986], 4). The Peoplehood of the Jews has been stressed regularly by Jewish participants in the theological dialogue between the Catholic Church and Jews. See the following examples: I. Jakobovits, Christian Jewish Relations, 16, 4 (1983), 18; M. Waxman, Address to Pope John Paul II as Chairman of ICIC, Christian Jewish Relations, 18, 4 (1985), 13; G. Wigoder, *A Jewish Reaction to the "Notes,"* J. Willebrands (ed.), Fifteen Years of Catholic Jewish Dialogue 1970–1985, 268. See also C. Thoma, A Christian Theology of Judaism (New York: Paulist, A Stimulus Book 1980), 167: *Summary of Statements of Jewish Identity;* D. Marmur, Beyond Survival (London: Darton Longman & Todd, 1982), xi–xviii, passim; E. Wiesel, A Jew Today (Canada: Villiers, 1979), 3–16, *To Be A Jew.*

61. Cf. E. Flannery, The Anguish of the Jews, 267–283. Flannery indicates these sources.

62. M. Saperstein, Moments of Crisis in Jewish-Christian Relations (London: SCM, 1989), 55.

IV. OFFICIAL CATHOLIC TEACHING
AND THE STATE OF ISRAEL

1. Cf. W. Abbott (ed.), The Documents of Vatican II (London: Chapman, 1966), 650–658.

2. Cf. F.G. Morrissey, *The Canonical Significance of Papal and Curial Pronouncements*, Canon Law Society of America, 10–11.

3. Morrissey, art. cit. 11–12.

4. Cf. Guidelines (1974), Preamble.

5. Cf. Guidelines (1974), Preliminary Considerations.

6. See The Code of Canon Law in English Translation (Bath: Pittman, 1983), Canon 753.

7. Cf. H. Vorgrimler, Commentary on the Documents of Vatican II, Volumes I–VI (London: Burns & Oates, 1967), Vol III, 40–41, *Decretum Judaeis*.

8. These prelates were: Cardinal Tappouni, Patriarch of the Syrian Rite of Antioch; Patriarch Stephanos I of Alexandria; Patriarch Maximos IV of Antioch (Melkite); the Latin Patriarch of Jerusalem, Alberto Gori; Peter XVI, Armenian Patriarch of Cilicia. A. Bea, The Church and the Jewish People, 23, relates how intent Pope John XXIII was on getting the "Jewish text" on the agenda and passed by the Council. In the face of mounting opposition the Pope sent a personal note to the Secretariat for Christian Unity in which he said, "*Having carefully examined Cardinal Bea's report, we unreservedly associate ourselves with the burden and responsibility of a concern which we must make our own*" (Bea, idem).

9. Cf. G. Baum, The Ecumenist 4, 2 (1966) 28; Bea, op. cit. 24–25; J. Oesterreicher, Vorgrimler, Commentary III, 48 and 49.

10. Cf. B. Hussar, *Nostra Aetate—20 Years Later,* Holy Land, VI, 2, Summer (1986), 65–75.

11. Bea, op. cit. 23–24; J. Oesterreicher, Vorgrimler, Commentary III, 86–90.

12. Some feared (Hussar, art. cit., 65ff) that this manner of finding a place for the uncomfortable "Jewish Document" had compromised its purpose. Bea and others tell us (Bea, op. cit. 25; Oesterreicher, ibid. 85) that it was seriously suggested at one stage that the "Jewish Document" be included in the *Dogmatic Constitution on the Church* (Lumen Gentium)—a more appropriate matrix for it than a document dealing with Buddhism, Islam and Animism. However, it is an ironical fact that throughout the Document's post-conciliar history, paragraph four has been treated with little or no regard to its immediate context. In fact the surrounding context appears to have become irrelevant since the Declaration's popular name Nostra Aetate is almost exclusively associated with paragraph four.

13. Cf. Oesterreicher, ibid. 101–136.

14. See Hussar, art. cit. 66, and Oesterreicher, ibid. 104–105, 117–122.

15. Bea, op. cit. 154–172.

16. Ibid. 159.

17. Ibid. 170. See also E.Y. Feldblum, The American Catholic Press and the Jewish State 1917–1959 (Jerusalem: Ktav, 1977), 109–117, who discusses the important supportive role which some American Catholic Bishops played in the passage of the document through the Council's procedures, and their work to steer it clear of political associations.

18. Cf. Oesterreicher, Vorgrimler, Commentary III, 123. For the pattern of voting, see Bea, op. cit. 24–26.

19. Cf. Bea, op. cit. 26.

20. See also Hussar, art. cit. 65.

21. Cf. Bea, op. cit. 154, 159, 164.

22. See Oesterreicher, Vorgrimler, Commentary III, 17–136, *The History of the Text.*

23. Ibid. 41, 42, 46, 75, 130, 131, 154.

24. Cf. F.G. Morrissey, art. cit. 7.

25. Ibid. 11–12.

26. Cf. Sacred Congregation for the Clergy, General Catechetical Directory (April 11, 1971), which incorporates special principles to be applied in catechesis.

27. Cf. Notes, Preliminary Considerations.

28. Cf. J. Mejia, *A Note for the Presentation of the Document of the Commission for Religious Relations with the Jews,* J. Willebrands (ed.), Fifteen Years of Catholic-Jewish Dialogue 1970–1985, 315.

29. Cf. Abbott, The Documents of Vatican II (1966), 665.

30. The framers of *Notes* refer to the Holocaust according to the dates of World War II, 1939–1945. This is incorrect. The systematic destruction of European Jewry began in 1933.

31. Cf. Notes, 25.

32. National Conference of Catholic Bishops, Statement on Catholic-Jewish Relations (November 1975).

33. See E. Fisher, *Implementing the Vatican Document "Notes on Jews and Judaism in Preaching and Catechesis,"* Living Light 22, 2 January (1986), 110.

34. Cf. E. Fisher, *The Holy See and the State of Israel: The Evaluation of Attitudes and Policies,* Journal of Ecumenical Studies, 24, 2 Spring (1987), 201.

35. Cf. H. Siegman, SIDIC VIII 3 (1975), 4–12. See also the Brockway-Fisher debate in Christian-Jewish Relations 18, 4 (1985), 18–54, 54–58. At the outset of this debate Brockway attempts to ascertain what Notes reflects of the Catholic Church's understanding of Jews and Judaism. He attempts to reflect on its contribution to Christian theology. He sees it, disappointedly, as being only a reference point for Christian theology, even as a focus for disagreement. Fisher's reply directs attention to the role of the document for Catholics, and the hermeneutical rules for interpreting such a document. He points out that it is not a theological treatise, as Brockway has apparently mistakenly taken it to be, and that it therefore leaves much unsaid. Fisher stresses that it must be read within the context of Vatican II and its papal statements and documents, the whole of which are evolving teaching.

36. Cf. E. Fisher, ibid. 191–211.

37. Cf. E. Fisher, *The Evaluation of Tradition,* Part One, SIDIC XIX 2 (1986), 9.

38. Cf. J. Mejia, *The Catholic Style: A Reflection on the Documents,* H. Croner (ed.), More Stepping Stones to Jewish-Christian Relations (New York: Paulist Press, 1985), 7–9.

39. Ibid. 8. Also note Mejia's comparison with liturgical changes, ibid. 9.

40. Cf. E. Fisher and L. Klenicki (eds.) (Washington DC: NCCB, 1987), Pope John Paul II on Jews and Judaism 1979–1986, where all of these allocutions have been collected and published. Because of the limited availability of this text, a list of all addresses, remarks and homilies, with dates and places, is supplied in Appendix A. The dates in the text above refer to the allocutions in Appendix A.

41. Ibid. 43–44, P. Klutznick, President of the World Jewish Congress.

42. Ibid. 23–26.

43. Ibid. 60, I. Jakobovits, Chief Rabbi of Great Britain and Northern Ireland.

44. Ibid. 44.

45. Ibid. 65, V. Goldbloom, President of the ICCI.

46. Ibid. 61.

47. Ibid. 70–78, H. Friedman, President of the American Jewish Committee.

48. Ibid. 68.

49. Fisher and Klenicki, op. cit. 53–57.

50. Cf. E. Fisher, Jewish Christian Relations, 18, 4 (1985), 54–58, who outlines the "hermeneutical rules" for interpreting the documents of the Holy See.

51. Cf. Fisher and Klenicki, op. cit. 56.

52. Cf. The Code of Canon Law in English Translation p. 65, Canon 368. Particular churches are principally dioceses under the jurisdiction of a Bishop. Sometimes groups of dioceses are referred to as "regional churches."

53. Cf. Appendix B.

54. Galveston-Houston (1975), H. Croner, More Stepping Stones to Jewish Christian Relations, 65. Los Angeles (1970), ibid. 74; Brooklyn (1979), ibid. 82; Cleveland (1979), ibid. 86; Austria (1979), SIDIC, IV 2 (1979), 42; Brazil, Croner, op. cit. 152.

55. A more intensive and wider dialogue: Los Angeles (1977), Croner, op. cit. 75; Brooklyn (1979), ibid. 80–81; Cleveland (1979), ibid. 86; Trenton (1980), ibid. 92–93; England and Wales, ibid. 120–122; Rome (1980), ibid. 146–147; Brazil (1984), ibid. 151.

56. The Debt Which Christians Owe to Jews: Galveston (1975), Croner, op. cit. 66–67; Cleveland (1979), ibid. 85–86; England and Wales (1980), ibid. 120–122; Bonn (1980), ibid. 131–137; Rome (1983), ibid. 146–147; Brazil (1984), ibid. 151.

57. Necessity To Explain Certain Attitudes in the Gospels: Detroit (1979), Croner, op. cit. 87–88.

58. Hope of Common Messianic Age: Bonn (1980), Croner, op. cit. 128–129; Brazil (1984), ibid. 153.

59. No Guilt for the Crucifixion: Galveston (1975), Croner, op. cit. 70; Detroit (1979) ibid. 87.

60. France (1973), SIDIC VI, 3 (1973), 38.

61. Austria (1979), SIDIC IV, 2 (1979), 42.

62. Cleveland (1975), Croner, op. cit. 86.

63. Galveston (1975), Croner, op. cit. 66; Detroit (1979), ibid. 90; Cleveland, ibid. 86; Brazil (1984), ibid. 153.

64. Ibid. 74 and 82–83.

65. Cf. Croner, op. cit. 85, para 2.

66. Detroit (1979).

67. Cleveland (1979), Croner, op. cit. 85.

68. National Conference of Catholic Bishops, Statement on Catholic-Jewish Relations (1975), E. Fisher, Faith Without Prejudice (New York: Paulist Press, 1977) 166.

69. National Conference of Catholic Bishops, Publication No 966 (Washington, D.C.: NCCB, 1985), 4–5.

70. Cf. Guidelines (1974), II, Liturgy, III, V.

71. Cf. French Guidelines, available as Document—Pastoral Orientation on the Attitudes of Christians to Judaism, SIDIC, VI, 2 (1973), 30–33.

72. Cf. Croner, op. cit. 142–144.

73. Ibid. 151–153.

74. R. Cohen, Rome and Jerusalem, Australia/Israel Review 4 18 October 10–24 (1979), 6–7.

75. C. Krauthammer, Australia/Israel Review 11, 6, 22 April—5 May (1986), 4. Reprinted from the International Herald Tribune.

76. Article 20 of the Palestinian National Covenant reads: "The claim of a historical or spiritual tie between Jews and Palestine does not tally with historical realities. . . . The Jews are not one people with an independent personality" (1964), quoted in Department of Information, World Zionist Organization, Anti-Zionism. A Threat to Israel, the Jewish People and Democracy (Jerusalem: W.Z.O., n.d.).

V. THE STATE OF ISRAEL AND CATHOLIC THEOLOGY

1. C. Klein, The Theological Dimensions of the State of Israel, Journal of Ecumenical Studies 10, 4 (1971), 700.

2. C. Rijk, Recent Developments: SIDIC Study Session: People, Land, Religion, SIDIC VIII, 2 (1975), 36.

3. C. Angell, Jews and Catholics Since Nostra Aetate, Christian Attitudes on Jews and Judaism, 46, February (1976), 15.

4. Notes on the Correct Way To Present Jews and Judaism (1985), VI, 25.

5. J. Oesterreicher, The Theologian and the Land, The Bridge Brothers in

Hope (New York: Herder, 1970) 321–243. A. T. Davies, art. cit. 56–60. I. De La Potterie and B. Dupuy, *People, Nation, Land: The Christian View,* I. Wille-brands (ed.), Fifteen Years of Catholic Jewish Dialogue 1970–1985 (Vatican: Libreria Editrice, 1988) 8–14. These authors are concerned with an exegesis of the terms "people," "nation," "land" in the Hebrew Scriptures. Their purpose is to review the biblical evidence in order to gain a view of these categories which Christians can absorb. C. Klein, art. cit. 700–715. C. A. Rijk, *People, Land and Religion,* SIDIC VIII, 2 (1975), 36–37. C. Thoma, *The Link Between People, Land and Religion in the Old and New Testaments.* SIDIC VIII, 2 (1975), 4–14. H. Hruby, *The Complexity of Contemporary Judaism,* SIDIC IX, 1 (1976), 4–12. T. Idinopoulos, *Zionism and Racism,* Christian Attitude to Jews and Judaism 47 April (1976), 5–9. C. Schoneveld, *The Religious Roots of Jewish Nationalism,* Christian Attitudes Toward Jews and Judaism, 46, February (1976), 1–7. E. Ecclestone, The Night Sky of the Lord (London: Longman, Darton and Todd, 1980), 168–188, Israel and the Nations. E. Fisher, *The Holocaust and the State of Israel: A Catholic Perspective,* Judaism 25, 1, Winter (1986), 16–24. W. Harrelson, The Land in Tanakh. An unpublished paper.

6. J. Parkes, The Emergence of the Jewish Problem (Harmondsworth: Pen-guin, 1956).

―――, End of Exile (London: Vallentine, Mitchell, 1954).

―――, Prelude to Dialogue (London: Vallentine, Mitchell, 1969).

―――, Whose Land? (Harmondsworth: Penguin, 1970). W. Brueggeman, The Land: Place as Gift, Promise and Challenge in Biblical Faith (Philadelphia: Fortress, 1977). Brueggeman's work attempts to contribute to contemporary redefinition of the category of "land" in biblical theology. The author's aim is to contribute to a current hermeneutical discussion and to probe the shape of the expectation biblical scholars have of the text. He is not concerned with the State of Israel as such.

7. Oesterreicher, op. cit. 241–243.

8. Davies, art. cit. 56–58.

9. C. Klein, art. cit. 701.

10. C. Rijk, art. cit. 36.

11. C. Thoma, art. cit. 4.

12. K. Hruby, art. cit. 4–5.

13. C. Schoneveld, art. cit. 2.

14. A. Ecclestone, op. cit. 173.

15. Fisher, art. cit. 9

16. B. Williams, art. cit. 33–34.

17. Cf. R. A. Everett, *A Christian Apology for Israel: A Study in the Thought of James Parkes,* Christian Jewish Relations 72 September (1980), 51.

18. J. Parkes, A History of the Jewish People (Harmondsworth: Penguin, 1964), 182.

19. W. Harrelson, art. cit. 1–4.

VI. MAJOR HURDLES FOR A CATHOLIC THEOLOGY
OF THE STATE OF ISRAEL

1. This program has been published: D. Cupitt, The Sea of Faith (London: BBC, 1985).

2. Cupitt, op. cit. 269.

3. Ibid. 271.

4. Cf., for instance, H. Croner, More Stepping Stones to Jewish-Christian Relations, who has collected and edited documentation from many Protestant churches, e.g. 161, *Third Revised Text of the British Working Group for the World Council of Churches Constitution on the Church and the Jewish People* (1977); 183, *The American Lutheran Church and the Jewish Community* (1982); 203, *Reflections of the Problem "Church-Israel," Central Board of the Union of Evangelical Churches;* 214, *Declaration of the Council of Churches in the Netherlands on Persistent Antisemitism.*

5. During the Jewish Revolt of the late 60s CE, there was an attempt by the Pharisees, now with their center at Javneh, under the leadership of Gamaliel II to bring factions within Judaism into a closer uniformity. To achieve this end the *minim* (heretics) had to be dealt with either by forcing them to conform or by expelling them from the Synagogue, which amounted to excommunication from Judaism. The means chosen was liturgical. An amendment was made to the *Shemoneh Esreh,* the Eighteen Benedictions known as "Amidah," literally "standing prayers." The aim of this change was to discover dissenters who would probably not recite the additional benediction which contained a curse against them and their leaders (cf. C.K. Barrett, The New Testament Background: Select Documents [London: SCM, 1974], 167, where a translation of the benediction is given). The wording of the prayer included Christians, called "followers of the Nazarene." This measure was in effect the beginning of the rift between Christians and Jews.

6. In the Letter to the Hebrews we find a fully developed annulment and replacement theology. The origins of this letter have been much debated. See G. Buchanan, To The Hebrews (New York: Doubleday, 1978), Anchor Bible, 263–267. The present writer does not hazard a guess as to authorship other than that it appears to be from the pen of a Jewish-Christian who has a thorough knowledge of the Jewish cultus and a great command of the Greek language. The present writer would argue that Hebrews is written after the destruction of the Jerusalem Temple in 70 C.E., and to a group of mourning, nostalgic Jewish-Christians who were possibly former priests of that Temple who had become Christians. It was written possibly to capture their faith in an entirely new order of realities which completely replace the "old." That is to say, the Temple with its priesthood, altar, and sacrifices has been entirely dispensed with and replaced by a new and everlasting temple, not made by human hands (Hebrews 8:1–3; 9:1–14); a new and eternal High Priest, infinitely superior in every way to the

old Levitical Priesthood (5:11–9:39); a new totally and eternally efficacious sacrifice and Covenant in the blood of Jesus the perfect High Priest (9:12, 14; 10:19, 29; 12:24; 13:20) once offered (9:26–28) whereby the first Covenant is abolished (8:7, 13). The new covenant fulfills Jeremiah 31 (8:8–12; 10:16) and puts away sins (9:14, 15, 25; 10:17–18).

7. This idea was first formulated in this manner by Origen (185–254) who wrote, "*Let no one therefore persuade himself or deceive himself: outside this house* (the Church) *no one is saved*" (On the Book of Joshua III.5). This idea was elaborated in a number of Fathers' works. We see it again in Cyprian (200–258), who uses the typological figure of Noah's Ark for the Church, but employs it in conjunction with the figure and imagery of the Song of Songs (4:12–13): "*A locked garden is my sister, my bride a sealed fountain, a living well of water.*" He concludes, "*Everyone who is 'outside' in heart is saved in the unity of the ark* (i.e. Gentiles), *by the same water by which everyone who is 'outside' in heart* (i.e. Jews and others) *perishes as an enemy of unity*" (On Baptism V, xxvii, 38–xxviii, 39). The same idea, with the figure of Noah's Ark is found in the writings of Jerome (345–42); see Letter 15, Ad Damasum. The same teaching resides in the Seventeenth Ecumenical Council (The Council of Florence), 1442, in its decree for the Jacobites (cf. H. Denzinger and A. Schonmetzer (eds.), Enchiridion Symbolorum Definitionum et Declarationum de Rebus Fidei et Morum XXXVI (Rome: Herder, 1974), 260, Doc. 802.

8. W. Abbott (ed.), The Documents of Vatican II (1966), *The Dogmatic Constitution on the Church in the Modern World,* #45, 247.

9. H. Bronstein, A Passover Haggadah (New York: CCAR, 1977), 34, *MAGGID,* The Narration. The same idea is expressed many times in the daily liturgical prayers; cf. S. Singer, Authorized Daily Prayer Book, passim.

10. For instance, in the two great "moments" of redemption, the Exodus and the death of Jesus. (1) The Exodus narrative, while stressing divine initiative throughout (e.g. Exodus 2:24–25; 3:7–12:17), and especially in the Victory Song at 15:1–18, equally portrays these events as "moments" of divine revelation, stressing this at such places as 3:1–6, 7–12, 13–15, 16–20. (2) The death of Jesus in the Christian Scriptures is seen as the supreme event of redemption (e.g. Mark 10:45 // Matthew 20:28 // Luke 22:24–27, and John 6:51; 10:11; 15:13; Romans 3:24; Galatians 3:13; 2 Corinthians 5:21), and also as the supreme "moment" of divine revelation (see, for instance, themes of the "hour" and "lifting up" of Jesus—all references to his death on the cross—which are developed together with the theme of his "glorification" in the Gospel of John. Thus, in these themes, culminating in the "glorification," the Fourth Evangelist portrays the supreme moment of divine revelation: 7:39; 8:54; 11:4; 12:6, 23, 28; 13:31, 32; 14:13; 15:8; 16:14; 17:1, 4, 5, 10. See also J.T. Forestall, The Word of the Cross (Rome: PBI, 1974), 2–57, who sees the evangelist's purpose as presenting Jesus—especially in his death on the cross—as a work of divine revelation.

11. Cf. Abbott, op. cit. 122, *Dogmatic Constitution on Divine Revelation,* 12.

12. Cf. (1) Matthew 3:2; 4:17; 12:28; 19:7; Mark 1:15; 11:10; Luke 10:9, 11; 11:20; 17:20; 19:11; 21:31. (2) The double aspect of the reign: Matthew 13; 18:23–35; 20:1–16; 25:1–13; Mark 4; Luke 8:4–18:13, 18–20.

13. For example, see Mark 13:26–32, 33–37; Matthew 24:29–30, 32–36, 37–44, 45–53; Luke 21:29–33, 34–36.

14. See M. Vogel, *The Link Between People, Land and Religion in Modern Thought,* SIDIC, VIII, 2 (1975), 15–32, who surveys modern Jewish thought in regard to Zionism. See also Chapter V above.

15. H. Fisch, The Zionist Revolution, 4–7.

16. Notes on the correct way to present Jews and Judaism, VI, 25.

VII. THE INTERNAL JEWISH DIALOGUE ON THE STATE OF ISRAEL

1. See, for example, C. Klein, *The Theological Dimensions of the State of Israel,* Journal of Ecumenical Studies 10, 4 (1971), 711, and E. Fisher, *The Holy See and the State of Israel: The Evolution of Attitudes and Policies,* Journal of Ecumenical Studies 24, 2 September (1987), 202.

2. Cf. Guidelines (1974), Preamble.

3. Cf. E. Fisher, Faith Without Prejudice, 166–167, NCCB, Statement on Catholic Jewish Relations.

4. Cf. W. Laqueur and B. Rubin (eds.), The Israel-Arab Reader, 11.

5. Cf. S. Singer (tr.), The Authorized Daily Prayer Book (London: Eyre & Spottiswood, 1984), 52; 107; 128; 158; 190; 240; 304; 331; 351.

6. Cf. H. Bronstein (ed.), A Passover Haggadah (New York: CCAR, 1977) 93, and S. Singer, op. cit. 366.

7. M. Hess, Rome and Jerusalem (New York: Philosophical Library, 1958), 66, Preface.

8. Ibid. 58, Fourth Letter.

9. R. Patai, The Messiah Texts (New York: Avon, 1979), 272, reproduced from R. Brainin, The Life of Theodor Herzl, 17–18.

10. In Eastern Europe the Jewish communities, bound by the Czarist government into concentrated and unassimilated existence, kept, on the whole, to their traditional structures and to their own cultures; cf. K. Hruby, *The Complexity of Contemporary Judaism,* SIDIC IX, 1, 1976, 8. See also S. Grayzel, A History of the Jewish People (Philadelphia: JPSA, 1968), 516–519, 520–528). Thus the Jewish Haskalah ("awakening," "enlightenment") in Eastern Europe was of a very different character to the Enlightenment for Jews of Western Europe. It was rooted in Hebrew language and culture, emphasizing Jewish history, theology and values. It was concerned to integrate Hebrew culture with its matrix culture rather than to throw Hebrew culture overboard in favor of secular culture.

11. Cf. W. Laqueer and B. Rubin (eds.), op. cit. 3–4.

12. Cf. S. Grayzel, A History of the Jewish People (Philadelphia: JPS, 1968), 497–515, and also M. Dimont, God, Jews and History (New York: NAL Penguin, 1962), 328–342.

13. Cf. Laqueer and Rubin, op. cit. 8–11.

14. Cf. Laqueer and Rubin, op. cit. 125–126.

15. Cf. H. Fisch, The Zionist Revolution (New York: St. Martin's, 1978), 83, 84, 85, 86, 179.

16. J.D. Haberman, "The Place of Israel in Reform Jewish Theology," Judaism 31, 4, Fall (1972), 439–460.

17. Ibid. 450

18. Ibid. 439

19. S. Schechter, Aspects of Rabbinical Theology (New York: Schocken, 1975), 114–115.

20. Ibid. 92.

21. Cf. F. Rosenzweig, The Star of Redemption (New York: Holt, Rinehart and Winston, 1971), 332. See the whole section, 331–335.

22. Cf. M. Buber, On Zion: The History of an Idea (Edinburgh: T & T Clark, 1985), 14.

23. The following divisions 1–5 are suggested by M. Vogel, *The Link Between People, Land and Religion in Modern Jewish Thought,* SIDIC VIII, 2 (1975), 15–32. Division 6 is a category added by the present author.

24. Cf. A. Hertzberg, The Zionist Idea (New York: Atheneum, 1986), 103–107; Y. Alkalai, *Kithe,* Vol. I. Jerusalem, 1945.

25. Ibid. 109–114, Cf. Z.H. Kalischer, *Derishat Tsiyyon.*

26. Cf. F. Rosenzweig, op. cit. 332.

27. Cf. Laqueur and Rubin, op. cit. 6–11; T. Herzl, *The Jewish State.*

28. Ibid. 235–245.

29. Cf. L. Pinsker, Auto-Emancipation (New York, 1944) (tr. D. Blondhcim).

30. Cf. A. Hertzberg, op. cit. 251–327; A. HaAm, *The Jewish State and the Jewish Problem* (tr. L. Simon); *Pades,* Vol. II. Odessa: n.a., 1894; *Hashiloah,* Vols. II and XIII, Krakov: n.a., 1904. See also L. Simon, Ahad HaAm: Selected Essays (Philadelphia, 1912), passim.

31. Cf. S. Dubnow, Babylon and Jerusalem (Massachusetts: London and Waltham, 1957).

32. Cf. M. Hess, Rome and Jerusalem, tr. M. Waxman.

33. The Bund was a Jewish socialist organization founded in Vienna in 1897. It was created primarily as a reaction to Zionist stirrings and through tensions within the Russian revolutionary movement. Its purpose was not a Jewish national one, but was to bring Jewish workers into the mainstream of the Russian revolution. Under the pressure of Socialist Zionists the Bund moved in the direction of accepting the separate culture of Jews as a lasting value worth preserving. Cf. A. Elon, The Israelis. Founders and Sons (New York: Holt, Rinehart and Winston, 1972), 59, 62–64.

34. Cf. A. Hertzberg, op. cit. 419–431; A.I. Kook, The Vision of Redemption (Jerusalem, 1941). See also Oroth (Jerusalem, 1950); Eretz Yisrael, Vol. II.

35. Cf. A.D. Gordon, Selected Essays, tr. F. Burnce (New York, 1938).

36. Cf. M. Buber, Israel and Palestine: The History of an Idea (London, 1968).

37. Cf. A. Hertzberg, op. cit. 548–555; M. Bar-Ilan, Kithe (Jerusalem, 1950).

38. Cf. A. Hertzberg, op. cit. 559–570; V. Jabotinsky, Evidence Submitted to the Palestine Royal Commission (pamphlet) (London, 1937).

39. Cf. C. Weizmann, Trial and Error (New York: Harper & Bros, 1949).

40. Cf. A.H. Silver, Vision and Victory (New York, 1949).

41. Cf. D. Ben Gurion, My Talks with Arab Leaders (Jerusalem, 1872); Rebirth and Destiny of Israel (New York, 1954); Years of Challenge (London, 1963).

42. A. Heschel, Israel: An Echo of Eternity. A Re-Examination, Face to Face IX, Fall (1982), 22.

43. Idem.

44. H. Fisch, The Zionist Revolution, 160.

45. U. Tal, The Relevance of Torah Today. The Land of Israel and the State of Israel in Israeli Religious Life, SIDIC X, 3 (1977), 4–15.

46. N. Rotenstreich, Secularism and Religion in Israel, Judaism 15, 3, Summer (1966), 259–283.

47. Y. Adam, Zionism and Judaism, Judaism 29, 3, Summer (1980), 279–285.

48. P. Eidelberg, Foundations of the State of Israel: An Analysis of Israel's Declaration of Independence, Judaism 36, 4, Fall (1987), 391–399.

49. S. Schafler, Modern Zionism—An Historic Perspective, Judaism 30, 1, Winter (1981), 111–119.

50. M. Langer, Democracy, Religion and the Zionist Future of Israel, Judaism 36, 4, Fall (1987), 400–415.

51. W.J. Fein, Israel or Zion? Judaism 22, 1, Winter (1973), 85–91.

52. N. Levine, The Jewish Revolution Is Not Complete, Judaism 23, 2, Spring (1974), 193–201.

53. C. Waxman, The Centrality of Israel in American Jewish Life: A Sociological Analysis, Judaism 25, 2, Spring (1976), 175–187.

54. B. Halpen, Exile and Redemption: A Secular Zionist View, Judaism 29, 2, Spring (1980), 177–184.

55. S. Schwartz, Redefining Zionism, Judaism 35, 3, Summer (1986), 316–334.

56. G. Tucker, Israel the Ever-Dying People, Judaism 37, 3, Summer (1988), 364–375.

57. This is not a homogeneous group, but factions within the ultra-Orthodox groupings, such as certain of the residents in Mea Shearim.

58. Mea Shearim, literally, "a hundred-fold," from Genesis 26:12—the stronghold in Western Jerusalem of Hasidic Orthodoxy since 1887.

59. Cf. A.J. Heschel, Israel: An Echo of Eternity (New York: Farrar, Strauss & Giroux, 1982), passim.

60. D. Marmur, Beyond Survival (London: Darton, Longman & Todd, 1982), 3–21.

61. C. Stern (ed.), Gates of Prayer. The New Union Prayer Book (New York: CCAR, 1985), 590–611.

62. Cf. Central Conference of American Rabbis, Yearbook, Vol. 80 (1970), 39.

63. H. Siegman, *Ten Years of Catholic-Jewish Relations: A Reassessment,* J. Willebrands (ed.), Fifteen Years of Catholic-Jewish Dialogue 1970–1985, 33.

64. Heschel, op. cit. 23.

VIII. CONCLUSION

1. Cf. E. Fisher, *The Holy See and the State of Israel: The Evaluation of Attitudes and Policies,* Journal of Ecumenical Studies 24, 2, Spring (1987), 201.

2. Idem.

3. Guidelines (1974), Preamble.

Index

Clemens Thoma and Michael Wyschogrod, editors, *Parable and Story in Judaism and Christianity* (A Stimulus Book, 1989).

Eugene J. Fisher and Leon Klenicki, editors, *In Our Time: The Flowering of Jewish-Catholic Dialogue* (A Stimulus Book, 1990).

Leon Klenicki, editor, *Toward a Theological Encounter* (A Stimulus Book, 1991).

David Burrell and Yehezkel Landau, editors, *Voices from Jerusalem* (A Stimulus Book, 1991).

John Rousmaniere, *A Bridge to Dialogue: The Story of Jewish-Christian Relations;* edited by James A. Carpenter and Leon Klenicki (A Stimulus Book, 1991).

Michael E. Lodahl, *Shekhinah/Spirit* (A Stimulus Book, 1992).

George M. Smiga, *Pain and Polemic: Anti-Judaism in the Gospels* (A Stimulus Book, 1992).

Eugene J. Fisher, editor, *Interwoven Destinies: Jews and Christians Through the Ages* (A Stimulus Book, 1993).

STIMULUS BOOKS are developed by Stimulus Foundation, a not-for-profit organization, and are published by Paulist Press. The Foundation wishes to further the publication of scholarly books on Jewish and Christian topics that are of importance to Judaism and Christianity.

Stimulus Foundation was established by an erstwhile refugee from Nazi Germany who intends to contribute with these publications to the improvement of communication between Jews and Christians.

Books for publication in this Series will be selected by a committee of the Foundation, and offers of manuscripts and works in progress should be addressed to:

Stimulus Foundation
785 West End Ave.
New York, N.Y. 10025